Company's Coming®

30-Minute
Weekday Meals

Jean Paré

www.companyscoming.com
visit our website

Front Cover

1. Antipasto Pizza, page 91
2. Cantonese Beef, page 12
3. Spicy Chicken And Salsa, page 32

Back Cover

1. Quickest Cioppino, page 43
2. Thai Chicken Noodle Soup, page 136
3. Lemon Lentil Soup, page 138

We gratefully acknowledge the following suppliers for their generous support of our Test and Photography Kitchens:

Broil King Barbecues	*Hamilton Beach® Canada*	*Proctor Silex® Canada*
Corelle®	*Lagostina®*	*Tupperware®*

30-Minute Weekday Meals

Eighth Printing March 2007

Library and Archives Canada Cataloguing in Publication
Paré, Jean, date
30-minute weekday meals / Jean Paré.
(Original series)
Includes index.
ISBN 13: 978-1-896891-75-0
1. Quick and easy cookery. 2. Suppers. I. Title. II. Title: Thirty-minute weekday meals.
III. Series: Paré, Jean, date. Original series.
TX833.5.P38 2005   641.5'55   C2004-907424-5

Published by
Company's Coming Publishing Limited
2311 – 96 Street
Edmonton, Alberta, Canada T6N 1G3
Tel: 780-450-6223   Fax: 780-450-1857
www.companyscoming.com

Company's Coming is a registered trademark owned by
Company's Coming Publishing Limited

Printed in Canada

Want cooking secrets?

Check out our website for ***cooking hints*** and ***time-saving shortcuts***.

Visit us at

www.companyscoming.com

Company's Coming Cookbooks

Original Series

- Softcover, 160 pages
- 6" x 9" (15 cm x 23 cm) format
- Lay-flat plastic comb binding
- Full-colour photos
- Nutrition information

Quick & easy recipes! Everyday ingredients!

Lifestyle Series

- Softcover, 160 pages
- 8" x 10" (20 cm x 25 cm) format
- Paperback
- Full-colour photos
- Nutrition information

Most Loved Recipe Collection

- Hardcover, 128 pages
- 8 3/4" x 8 3/4" (22 cm x 22 cm) format
- Durable sewn binding
- Full-colour throughout
- Nutrition information

Special Occasion Series

- Hardcover & softcover
- 8 1/2" x 11" (22 cm x 28 cm) format
- Durable sewn binding
- Full-colour throughout
- Nutrition information

See page 157 for more cookbooks.
For a complete listing, visit
www.companyscoming.com

Table of Contents

The Company's Coming Story

Jean Paré (pronounced "jeen PAIR-ee") grew up understanding that the combination of family, friends and home cooking is the best recipe for a good life. From her mother, she learned to appreciate good cooking, while her father praised even her earliest attempts in the kitchen. When Jean left home, she took with her a love of cooking, many family recipes and an intriguing desire to read cookbooks as if they were novels!

"never share a recipe you wouldn't use yourself"

In 1963, when her four children had all reached school age, Jean volunteered to cater the 50th Anniversary of the Vermilion School of Agriculture, now Lakeland College, in Alberta, Canada. Working out of her home, Jean prepared a dinner for more than 1,000 people, which launched a flourishing catering operation that continued for over 18 years. During that time, she had countless opportunities to test new ideas with immediate feedback—resulting in empty plates and contented customers! Whether preparing cocktail sandwiches for a house party or serving a hot meal for 1,500 people, Jean Paré earned a reputation for good food, courteous service and reasonable prices.

As requests for her recipes mounted, Jean was often asked the question, "Why don't you write a cookbook?" Jean responded by teaming up with her son, Grant Lovig, in the fall of 1980 to form Company's Coming Publishing Limited. The publication of *150 Delicious Squares* on April 14, 1981 marked the debut of what would soon become one of the world's most popular cookbook series.

The company has grown since those early days when Jean worked from a spare bedroom in her home. Today, she continues to write recipes while working closely with the staff of the Recipe Factory, as the Company's Coming test kitchen is affectionately known. There she fills the role of mentor, assisting with the development of recipes people most want to use for everyday cooking and easy entertaining. Every Company's Coming recipe is *kitchen-tested* before it's approved for publication.

Jean's daughter, Gail Lovig, is responsible for marketing and distribution, leading a team that includes sales personnel located in major cities across Canada. In addition, Company's Coming cookbooks are published and distributed under licence in the United States, Australia and other world markets. Bestsellers many times over in English, Company's Coming cookbooks have also been published in French and Spanish.

Familiar and trusted in home kitchens around the world, Company's Coming cookbooks are offered in a variety of formats. Highly regarded as kitchen workbooks, the softcover Original Series, with its lay-flat plastic comb binding, is still a favourite among readers.

Jean Paré's approach to cooking has always called for *quick and easy recipes* using *everyday ingredients*. That view has served her well. The recipient of many awards, including the Queen Elizabeth Golden Jubilee medal, Jean was appointed a Member of the Order of Canada, her country's highest lifetime achievement honour.

Jean continues to gain new supporters by adhering to what she calls The Golden Rule of Cooking: *"Never share a recipe you wouldn't use yourself."* It's an approach that works—*millions of times over!*

Foreword

If you're like me, there are days when you don't mind spending several hours preparing a meal—but not always, and certainly not on busy weekdays. Whether choice or circumstance means dinner has to come together quickly and smoothly, we all know that having a plan makes all the difference.

In *30-Minute Weekday Meals,* we did all the planning so you can just get to it. Choose a recipe and know that 30 minutes later your family will be sitting down to a wonderful home-cooked meal.

By using the shortcuts we've listed on page 8, preparing your ingredients first and multi-tasking where possible, half an hour is all the time you need to chop the vegetables, measure the ingredients and cook the food!

You'll be surprised at how easy it is to make tasty tacos, perfect pizzas or fluffy frittatas. A platter of pasta, batch of burritos, even a pot of stew can be on the table faster than you'd expect. Stir-frying is a great way to save time and serve flavourful meals. Salads, soups and sandwiches are always good to keep in mind. A crisp, fresh meal salad is ready in a jiffy. And one of life's best eat-and-go meals is a bowl of hot, savoury soup with a special homemade sandwich. Every one of these recipes lets you feed your family without a lot of fuss.

And to make your life even easier, check out the Make It A Meal suggestions with each recipe—great ideas to make a balanced meal using everyday ingredients. And it's ready within the same 30 minutes it takes to do the recipe!

We've also offered suggestions for a Pantry List on page 9—a list of convenient foods for these recipes to keep on hand in your cupboard, refrigerator or freezer. You can also use recently refrigerated or frozen and thawed leftovers to save even more time.

On those days when you'd rather spend time sharing a meal instead of making it, enjoy a family dinner in short order with *30-Minute Weekday Meals.*

Jean Paré

Nutrition Information Guidelines

Each recipe is analyzed using the most current version of the Canadian Nutrient File from Health Canada, which is based on the United States Department of Agriculture (USDA) Nutrient Database.

- If more than one ingredient is listed (such as "hard margarine or butter"), or if a range is given (1 – 2 tsp., 5 – 10 mL), only the first ingredient or first amount is analyzed.

- For meat, poultry and fish, the serving size per person is based on the recommended 4 oz. (113 g) uncooked weight (without bone), which is 2 – 3 oz. (57 – 85 g) cooked weight (without bone)— approximately the size of a deck of playing cards.

- Milk used is 1% M.F. (milk fat), unless otherwise stated.

- Cooking oil used is canola oil, unless otherwise stated.

- Ingredients indicating "sprinkle," "optional," or "for garnish" are not included in the nutrition information.

Margaret Ng, B.Sc. (Hon.), M.A.
Registered Dietitian

Hints For Quick Meal Preparation

- Read the recipe through completely. Do ingredient preparation work first, or even ahead of time.

- Multi-task where possible. For example, while the noodles are boiling or the meat is cooking, chop the vegetables or prepare a salad.

- Cook in the microwave, a wok, on a two-sided grill or on a barbecue to save time.

- Wash produce before storing in the refrigerator so it's ready when needed.

- To thaw frozen ingredients, put them in the refrigerator for the day, defrost them in the microwave, or hold them under running water.

- Keep a weekly shopping list of things needed from the grocery store to make the most out of each trip. This will keep cupboards stocked to help save time.

- Use convenience foods such as sliced mushrooms, grated or sliced cheese, prewashed and packaged spinach and mixed greens, precooked bacon, and frozen or canned vegetables and fruit.

- Buy a jar of minced garlic in oil. Substitute 1 tsp. (5 mL) for each garlic clove. Keep chilled after opening to maintain freshness.

- Buy dried herbs for easy flavouring and store in a cool, dark place.

- Keep toasted nuts in the freezer for easy addition to recipes.

- Buy chicken or fish pieces in bulk. Season and arrange them in a single layer on a baking sheet. Freeze. Remove to large resealable freezer bag. Remove individual pieces as needed.

- Buy fresh lean ground beef, chicken or turkey in bulk. Season and shape into patties. Place in a single layer in a large resealable freezer bag in one-meal portions. Flatten the bag, pressing out all the air so the packages will stack neatly. One-meal portions will shorten thawing time.

- Make leftovers intentionally. Cook larger portions of meat, rice, pasta or vegetables on the weekend to use during the week. Freeze leftovers in large resealable freezer bags or airtight containers.

- Keep a large resealable freezer bag or large airtight container in the freezer for soup ingredients. Add leftovers such as carrots, pasta, potatoes or meat once they have cooled to room temperature. When the bag or container is full, heat the leftovers with soup stock or prepared broth.

- Keep an airtight container for chili in the freezer. Add leftovers such as taco meat, other cooked meats or spaghetti sauce once they have cooled to room temperature. When the container is full, heat the leftovers with baked beans, vegetables or tomato sauce.

Pantry List

Staples such as flour, eggs, sugar, butter, rice, pasta and a variety of canned and frozen goods are likely already in your cupboard, refrigerator or freezer. To make sure you are pantry-ready to make most of the recipes in *30-Minute Weekday Meals,* you might want to have some of these frequently called-for or less common ingredients on hand as well.

In your cupboard

- Bouillon powder (beef & chicken)

- Canned goods:
  Black beans
  Chickpeas
  Crabmeat
  Diced tomatoes
  Evaporated milk
  Lentils
  Mandarin orange segments
  Mixed beans
  Prepared broth (beef, chicken & vegetable)
  Tomato paste
  Vegetables (a variety)

- Croutons

- Dried cranberries

- Juices

- Liquid honey

- Maple (or maple-flavoured) syrup

- Oriental noodles:
  Chinese egg
  Chow mein
  Shanghai
  Steam-fried

- Polenta (ready-made)

- Sauces:
  Pasta
  Pizza
  Tomato
  Worcestershire

In your refrigerator

- Bacon (precooked)

- Cheeses:
  Cheddar
  Grated Parmesan
  Mozzarella

- Dijon mustard

- Lemon (or lime) juice

- Mayonnaise

- Pesto

- Salsa

- Salad dressings (a variety)

- Sauces:
  Ketchup
  Regular chili
  Soy
  Sweet chili
  Teriyaki

- Sweet pickles

- Vinegars:
  Balsamic
  Red wine
  White

In your freezer

- Breads:
  Garlic
  Hamburger buns
  Pita
  Pizza crusts (prebaked)
  Tortillas

- Meat, Poultry & Seafood:
  Meatballs (ready-made)
  Sausage (a variety)
  Shrimp skewers (ready-made)
  Various cuts

- Toasted nuts & seeds

- Concentrated orange juice

- Perogies

- Potatoes (French fries, hash browns, wedges, etc.)

- Spring rolls or egg rolls

- Vegetables (a variety)

Beef Noodle Skillet

A one-dish meal that's great for a quick family dinner.

Cooking oil	1 tsp.	5 mL
Lean ground beef	1 lb.	454 g
Seasoned salt	1 tsp.	5 mL
Pepper	1/2 tsp.	2 mL
Can of diced tomatoes (with juice)	14 oz.	398 mL
Can of vegetable cocktail juice (such as V8 juice)	12 oz.	340 mL
Water	1 cup	250 mL
Penne (or other tube) pasta (about 8 oz., 225 g)	2 2/3 cups	650 mL
Frozen mixed vegetables, thawed	1 cup	250 mL
Sour cream	1 cup	250 mL
Grated Parmesan cheese	1/4 cup	60 mL
Chopped green onion	2 tbsp.	30 mL

Heat cooking oil in large frying pan on medium-high. Add ground beef, seasoned salt and pepper. Scramble-fry for 5 to 10 minutes until beef is no longer pink. Drain.

Add next 3 ingredients. Stir.

Add pasta and vegetables. Stir well. Bring to a boil. Reduce heat to medium. Cover. Simmer for about 18 minutes, stirring occasionally, until pasta is tender but firm.

Add remaining 3 ingredients. Heat and stir for about 1 minute until heated through. Serves 4.

1 serving: 583 Calories; 22.5 g Total Fat (8 g Mono, 1.7 g Poly, 10.6 g Sat); 88 mg Cholesterol; 60 g Carbohydrate; 4 g Fibre; 35 g Protein; 999 mg Sodium

Pictured on page 18.

Make It A Meal with a salad of fresh spinach leaves, sliced mushrooms and thinly sliced red onion tossed with your favourite creamy dressing.

Quick Chili

A tasty dish that's fast and easy
Garnish with Cheddar to make it cheesy!
A bit of heat and lots of flavour
A perfect answer to "What's for dinner?"

Cooking oil	1 tsp.	5 mL
Lean ground beef	1 lb.	454 g
Chopped onion	1/2 cup	125 mL
Chili powder	1 tbsp.	15 mL
Ground cumin	1 tsp.	5 mL
Granulated sugar	1 tsp.	5 mL
Dried basil	1/2 tsp.	2 mL
Dried crushed chilies	1/2 tsp.	2 mL
Salt	1/2 tsp.	2 mL
Can of diced tomatoes (with juice)	14 oz.	398 mL
Can of red kidney beans, rinsed and drained	14 oz.	398 mL
Can of tomato sauce	7 1/2 oz.	213 mL

Heat cooking oil in large frying pan on medium-high. Add ground beef and onion. Scramble-fry for 5 to 10 minutes until beef is no longer pink and onion is softened. Drain.

Add next 6 ingredients. Heat and stir for about 1 minute until fragrant.

Add remaining 3 ingredients. Stir well. Bring to a boil. Reduce heat to medium. Simmer, uncovered, for about 5 minutes, stirring occasionally, until heated through. Serves 4.

1 serving: 311 Calories; 11.7 g Total Fat (4.9 g Mono, 1 g Poly, 3.9 g Sat); 59 mg Cholesterol; 26 g Carbohydrate; 7 g Fibre; 28 g Protein; 995 mg Sodium

Pictured on page 18.

Make It A Meal with crisp tortilla chips and buttered corn on the cob.

Cantonese Beef

*A rich ginger sauce makes this beef and vegetable stir-fry
something special. A dish the whole family will love!*

Dry sherry	1 tbsp.	15 mL
Cornstarch	1 tsp.	5 mL
Oyster sauce	2 tbsp.	30 mL
Soy sauce	1 tbsp.	15 mL
Brown sugar, packed	1 tbsp.	15 mL
Minced pickled ginger slices, drained (or 1/2 tsp., 2 mL, finely grated, peeled gingerroot)	1 tsp.	5 mL
Cooking oil	1 tbsp.	15 mL
Can of cut baby corn, drained	14 oz.	398 mL
Snow peas, trimmed	1 1/2 cups	375 mL
Fresh whole white mushrooms	1 1/2 cups	375 mL
Green onions, cut into 1 inch (2.5 cm) pieces	4	4
Cooking oil	1 tbsp.	15 mL
Beef tenderloin steak, cut across grain into 1/8 inch (3 mm) slices, then halved (see Tip, page 13)	3/4 lb.	340 g

Stir sherry into cornstarch in small cup until smooth. Add next
4 ingredients. Stir. Set aside.

Heat wok or large frying pan on medium-high until very hot. Add first
amount of cooking oil. Add next 4 ingredients. Stir-fry for about 2 minutes
until snow peas are tender-crisp. Transfer to large bowl.

Heat second amount of cooking oil in same wok. Add beef. Stir-fry for
about 2 minutes until desired doneness. Add vegetables. Stir. Stir
cornstarch mixture. Add to beef mixture. Heat and stir for about 1 minute
until sauce is boiling and slightly thickened and vegetables are heated
through. Serves 4.

*1 serving: 302 Calories; 14 g Total Fat (6.5 g Mono, 2.6 g Poly, 2.9 g Sat); 43 mg Cholesterol;
24 g Carbohydrate; 3 g Fibre; 22 g Protein; 945 mg Sodium*

Pictured on front cover.

Make It A Meal with hot long grain rice sprinkled with toasted
sesame seeds.

Beef

Skillet Shepherd's Pie

Get out the skillet, there's onion to fry.
Chop it up quickly and try not to cry.
A little of that and a little of this—
You'll hit a home run they'll not want to miss.
Sprinkle with parsley now, just for some fun.
A mere 30 minutes and dinner is done!

Cooking oil	1 tsp.	5 mL
Lean ground beef	1 lb.	454 g
Chopped onion	1/2 cup	125 mL
Can of potatoes, drained and cut up	19 oz.	540 mL
Can of kernel corn (with liquid)	12 oz.	341 mL
Can of condensed cream of chicken soup	10 oz.	284 mL
Sour cream	1 cup	250 mL
Jar of pimiento, well-drained and chopped	2 oz.	57 mL
Salt	3/4 tsp.	4 mL
Pepper	1/4 tsp.	1 mL

Chopped fresh parsley, for garnish

Heat cooking oil in large frying pan on medium. Add ground beef and onion. Scramble-fry for 5 to 10 minutes until beef is no longer pink and onion is softened. Drain.

Add next 7 ingredients. Heat and stir for 5 to 7 minutes until heated through. Remove to large serving dish.

Garnish with parsley. Serves 4.

1 serving: 447 Calories; 24 g Total Fat (9.3 g Mono, 2.2 g Poly, 10.4 g Sat); 88 mg Cholesterol; 32 g Carbohydrate; 3 g Fibre; 27 g Protein; 1458 mg Sodium

Make It A Meal with a mixed green salad and tomato wedges drizzled with a tangy herb vinaigrette.

 To slice meat easily, freeze for about 30 minutes. If using frozen, partially thaw before slicing.

Orange Beef Stir-Fry

Oranges and broccoli glisten in a mild ginger sauce.
This is sure to disappear quickly!

Orange juice	1/4 cup	60 mL
Soy sauce	1 tbsp.	15 mL
Liquid honey	1 tbsp.	15 mL
Cornstarch	2 tsp.	10 mL
Garlic clove, minced (or 1/4 tsp., 1 mL, powder)	1	1
Grated orange zest	1 tsp.	5 mL
Finely grated, peeled gingerroot (or 1/4 tsp., 1 mL, ground ginger)	1 tsp.	5 mL
Cooking oil	2 tsp.	10 mL
Beef top sirloin steak, cut diagonally across grain into thin slices (see Tip, page 13)	1 lb.	454 g
Cooking oil	1 tsp.	5 mL
Broccoli florets	1 1/2 cups	375 mL
Green onions, cut into 1 inch (2.5 cm) pieces	6	6
Medium oranges, peeled, segmented, chopped	2	2

Combine first 7 ingredients in small bowl. Set aside.

Heat wok or large frying pan on medium-high until very hot. Add first amount of cooking oil. Add beef. Stir-fry for about 2 minutes until desired doneness. Transfer to small bowl. Cover to keep warm.

Heat second amount of cooking oil in same wok on medium. Add broccoli and green onion. Stir-fry for about 2 minutes until broccoli is bright green.

Add beef and chopped orange. Stir. Stir cornstarch mixture. Add to beef mixture. Heat and stir for about 2 minutes until sauce is boiling and thickened and broccoli is tender-crisp. Serves 4.

1 serving: 292 Calories; 13.8 g Total Fat (6.4 g Mono, 1.5 g Poly, 4.3 g Sat); 56 mg Cholesterol; 19 g Carbohydrate; 1 g Fibre; 24 g Protein; 334 mg Sodium

Make It A Meal with hot long grain rice sprinkled with sesame seeds.

Beef

Potato-Crowned Steaks

A fancier presentation than usual, but easily put together.
Choose steaks of even thickness for best results.

Grated, peeled potato, blotted dry	1 cup	250 mL
Grated red onion, blotted dry	1/2 cup	125 mL
All-purpose flour	1/4 cup	60 mL
Large egg, fork-beaten	1	1
Grated Parmesan cheese	2 tbsp.	30 mL
Parsley flakes	1 tsp.	5 mL
Paprika	1/4 tsp.	1 mL
Salt	1/2 tsp.	2 mL
Pepper	1/8 tsp.	0.5 mL
Cooking oil	2 tsp.	10 mL
Beef tenderloin steaks (4 – 6 oz., 113 – 170 g and at least 1 inch, 2.5 cm, thick, each)	4	4
Salt, sprinkle		
Pepper, sprinkle		
Cooking oil	2 tsp.	10 mL

Preheat oven to 500°F (260°C). Combine first 9 ingredients in medium bowl.

Heat first amount of cooking oil in large frying pan on medium-high. Sprinkle both sides of each steak with second amounts of salt and pepper. Add steaks to pan. Cook for about 1 minute per side until browned. Transfer to large plate. Spread potato mixture evenly on top of each steak.

Heat second amount of cooking oil in same large frying pan. Add steaks, potato-side down. Cook for about 1 minute until potato mixture is golden. Transfer steaks, potato-side up, to greased baking sheet. Bake for 8 to 10 minutes until desired doneness. Serves 4.

1 serving: 317 Calories; 15 g Total Fat (6.6 g Mono, 2 g Poly, 4.4 g Sat); 113 mg Cholesterol; 16 g Carbohydrate; 1 g Fibre; 28 g Protein; 436 mg Sodium

Make It A Meal with steamed and buttered asparagus spears sprinkled with lemon pepper for an added flavour burst.

Tomato Pesto Steak

Fire up the barbecue and enjoy this grilled steak and tangy Pesto Sauce.

Sun-dried tomato pesto	2 tbsp.	30 mL
Cooking oil	1 tsp.	5 mL
Strip loin steak, cut into 4 equal portions	1 lb.	454 g
PESTO SAUCE		
Mayonnaise	1/4 cup	60 mL
Sun-dried tomato pesto	2 tbsp.	30 mL
Garlic clove, minced (or 1/4 tsp., 1 mL, powder)	1	1

Preheat electric grill for 5 minutes or gas barbecue to medium-high (see Note). Combine pesto and cooking oil in small cup. Spread evenly on both sides of each steak portion. Cook on greased grill for 4 to 5 minutes per side until desired doneness. Remove to large serving plate. Cover with foil. Let stand for 5 minutes. Meanwhile, prepare Pesto Sauce.

Pesto Sauce: Combine all 3 ingredients in small bowl. Makes about 1/3 cup (75 mL) sauce. Serve with steak. Serves 4.

1 serving: 395 Calories; 32 g Total Fat (15.6 g Mono, 4.9 g Poly, 8.9 g Sat); 69 mg Cholesterol; 2 g Carbohydrate; 0 g Fibre; 24 g Protein; 149 mg Sodium

Pictured on page 17.

Note: Steak may be broiled in oven. Place on greased broiler pan. Broil about 4 inches (10 cm) from heat in oven for about 4 minutes per side until desired doneness.

Make It A Meal with zucchini slices and red pepper quarters. Brush both sides with olive oil and sprinkle with salt and pepper. Grill alongside steak. Serve with garlic toast.

1. Tomato Pesto Steak, above
2. Blue Cheese Buttered Steak, page 21

Props courtesy of: Casa Bugatti
Pfaltzgraff Canada

Beef

Pesto Pizza

Just as fast as ordering in, and full of zesty pesto flavour.
For a different taste, use ham, salami or pepperoni instead of beef.

Tube of refrigerator pizza dough	10 oz.	283 g
Basil pesto	1/4 cup	60 mL
Chopped deli roast beef (see Note)	1/2 cup	125 mL
Chopped tomato	1/4 cup	60 mL
Can of sliced ripe olives, drained	4 1/2 oz.	125 mL
Goat (chèvre) cheese, cut up	4 oz.	113 g
Grated part-skim mozzarella cheese	1/2 cup	125 mL
Pepper	1/2 tsp.	2 mL

Preheat oven to 425°F (220°C). Unroll and press pizza dough in greased 10 × 15 inch (25 × 38 cm) baking sheet with sides or 12 inch (30 cm) pizza pan, forming rim around edge. Spread pesto evenly on dough.

Scatter next 5 ingredients, in order given, over pesto.

Sprinkle with pepper. Bake for about 15 minutes until cheese is melted and crust is golden. Cuts into 8 pieces.

1 piece: 212 Calories; 10.6 g Total Fat (3.9 g Mono, 0.4 g Poly, 4.5 g Sat); 22 mg Cholesterol; 18 g Carbohydrate; 1 g Fibre; 11 g Protein; 336 mg Sodium

Pictured on page 36.

Note: Use leftover roast beef instead of deli beef.

Make It A Meal with a salad of crisp lettuce greens, thinly sliced celery and cucumber tossed with a peppercorn dressing.

1. Quick Chili, page 11
2. Beef Noodle Skillet, page 10

Props courtesy of: Cherison Enterprises Inc.
Danesco Inc.

Pepper Steak Sandwiches

Green peppercorns add zip to tangy, tomato sauce.
An appetizing open-face sandwich.

Water	2 tbsp.	30 mL
Cornstarch	2 tbsp.	30 mL
Cooking oil	1 tsp.	5 mL
Rib-eye steaks, cut in half lengthwise, then crosswise into 1/2 inch (12 mm) slices (see Tip, page 13)	1 lb.	454 g
Cooking oil	1 tsp.	5 mL
Can of diced tomatoes, drained	14 oz.	398 mL
Sliced fresh white mushrooms	1 cup	250 mL
Chopped green pepper	1/2 cup	125 mL
Chopped onion	1/2 cup	125 mL
Garlic clove, minced (or 1/4 tsp., 1 mL, powder)	1	1
Dry red (or alcohol-free) wine	1/4 cup	60 mL
Prepared beef broth	2 cups	500 mL
Whole green peppercorns, drained	1 tbsp.	15 mL
Dried thyme	1 tsp.	5 mL
Thick French bread slices	4	4

Stir water into cornstarch in small cup until smooth. Set aside.

Heat first amount of cooking oil in large frying pan on medium-high. Add steak. Cook for about 5 minutes, stirring occasionally, until browned. Transfer to small bowl. Cover to keep warm.

Heat second amount of cooking oil in same large frying pan. Add next 5 ingredients. Heat and stir for about 3 minutes until green pepper is tender-crisp.

Add wine. Heat and stir for 1 minute.

Add next 3 ingredients. Stir. Bring to a boil. Reduce heat to medium. Boil gently, uncovered, for 10 minutes, stirring occasionally, to blend flavours. Stir cornstarch mixture. Add to vegetable mixture. Add steak. Heat and stir for 1 to 2 minutes until sauce is boiling and thickened. Remove from heat. Cover to keep warm.

(continued on next page)

Beef

Toast bread slices. Place 1 toast slice on each of 4 plates. Spoon steak mixture onto each. Serves 4.

1 serving: 459 Calories; 22.5 g Total Fat (9.9 g Mono, 1.8 g Poly, 8.1 g Sat); 60 mg Cholesterol; 32 g Carbohydrate; 3 g Fibre; 29 g Protein; 855 mg Sodium

Make It A Meal with frozen french fries cooked according to package directions and a Caesar salad kit (available in your grocer's produce department).

Blue Cheese Buttered Steak

Rich, flavourful blue cheese butter melts invitingly over grilled steak.

Blue cheese	2 tbsp.	30 mL
Butter (not margarine), softened	2 tbsp.	30 mL
Dijon mustard	1/2 tsp.	2 mL
Worcestershire sauce	1/4 tsp.	1 mL
Small garlic clove, minced (or 1/8 tsp., 0.5 mL, powder)	1	1
Rib-eye steak, cut into 4 equal portions	1 lb.	454 g
Pepper, sprinkle		

Preheat electric grill for 5 minutes or gas barbecue to medium-high (see Note). Combine first 5 ingredients in small bowl. Spoon onto sheet of waxed paper. Shape into 2 inch (5 cm) long log. Wrap with waxed paper. Place in freezer until ready to serve.

Sprinkle both sides of each steak portion with pepper. Cook on greased grill for 5 to 6 minutes per side until desired doneness. Transfer to large plate. Cover with foil. Let stand for 5 minutes. Meanwhile, unwrap blue cheese log. Cut into 4 equal pieces. Place 1 steak portion on each of 4 plates. Top each with 1 blue cheese butter slice. Serves 4.

1 serving: 333 Calories; 25.6 g Total Fat (10.1 g Mono, 0.9 g Poly, 11.9 g Sat); 79 mg Cholesterol; 1 g Carbohydrate; 0 g Fibre; 24 g Protein; 183 mg Sodium

Pictured on page 17.

Note: Steak may be broiled in oven. Place on greased broiler pan. Broil about 4 inches (10 cm) from heat in oven for about 5 minutes per side until desired doneness.

Make It A Meal with sweet potato and zucchini slices. Brush both sides with olive oil and sprinkle with seasoned salt. Grill alongside steak.

Chipotle Chili Tacos

Spicy beef-and-bean filling makes these crunchy tacos especially tasty.
Add another chili pepper if your family likes more heat.

Cooking oil	1 tbsp.	15 mL
Lean ground beef	3/4 lb.	340 g
Can of red kidney beans, rinsed and drained	14 oz.	398 mL
Salsa	1/2 cup	125 mL
Chipotle chili pepper, chopped (see Tip, page 23)	1	1
Sweet (or regular) chili sauce	2 tbsp.	30 mL
Taco seasoning mix, stir before measuring	2 tbsp.	30 mL
Water	2 tbsp.	30 mL
Hard taco shells	12	12

Preheat oven according to taco shell package directions. Heat cooking oil in large frying pan on medium-high. Add ground beef. Scramble-fry for 5 to 10 minutes until no longer pink. Drain.

Add next 6 ingredients. Stir. Reduce heat to medium. Cook, uncovered, for about 5 minutes, stirring occasionally, until heated through.

Meanwhile, heat taco shells in oven. Place shells in large serving dish. Spoon beef mixture into each shell. Makes 12 tacos.

1 taco: 152 Calories; 6.7 g Total Fat (3 g Mono, 1.6 g Poly, 1.5 g Sat); 15 mg Cholesterol; 16 g Carbohydrate; 3 g Fibre; 8 g Protein; 501 mg Sodium

Pictured on page 54.

Make It A Meal with toppings such as shredded lettuce, grated Cheddar cheese, sour cream and chopped tomato. Put in separate small bowls and serve with tacos.

Paré Pointer

To find a spider on your computer, simply check out its website.

Sausage, Spinach And Feta

A colourful combination with lots of sauce for pasta or potatoes.
Use hot Italian or chorizo sausage, for a change of taste.

Cooking oil	1 tsp.	5 mL
Beef sausages, cut into 1/2 inch (12 mm) slices	1 1/4 lbs.	560 g
Olive (or cooking) oil	1 tbsp.	15 mL
Chopped red onion	1 cup	250 mL
Fresh spinach leaves, lightly packed	4 cups	1 L
Chopped tomato	3 cups	750 mL
Dried basil	1 1/2 tsp.	7 mL
Crumbled feta cheese (about 2 1/2 oz., 70 g)	1/2 cup	125 mL
Pepper	1/4 tsp.	1 mL

Heat cooking oil in large frying pan on medium. Add sausage. Cook for about 10 minutes, stirring occasionally, until no longer pink. Transfer with slotted spoon to paper towels to drain. Discard drippings.

Heat olive oil in same large frying pan. Add onion. Cook for 5 to 10 minutes, stirring often, until softened.

Add spinach, tomato and basil. Heat and stir for about 2 minutes until spinach starts to wilt.

Add sausage, cheese and pepper. Heat and stir for about 2 minutes until heated through and cheese is almost melted. Serves 4.

1 serving: 395 Calories; 32 g Total Fat (14.7 g Mono, 3.2 g Poly, 12 g Sat); 64 mg Cholesterol; 14 g Carbohydrate; 4 g Fibre; 15 g Protein; 810 mg Sodium

Make It A Meal with hot, buttered fettuccine or mashed potatoes. Or for something different, try steamed spaghetti squash.

Chilies and hot peppers contain capsaicin in the seeds and ribs. Removing the seeds and ribs will reduce the heat. Wear rubber gloves when handling chilies or peppers and avoid touching your eyes. Wash your hands well afterwards.

One-Dish Lazy Enchiladas

Zesty chili flavour in a layered skillet dinner. A no-fuss way to enjoy enchiladas.

Cooking oil	1 tsp.	5 mL
Lean ground beef	1 lb.	454 g
Chopped onion	1 1/4 cups	300 mL
All-purpose flour	1 tbsp.	15 mL
Can of stewed tomatoes (with juice)	14 oz.	398 mL
Salsa	1 1/2 cups	375 mL
Can of diced green chilies (do not drain)	4 oz.	113 g
Garlic salt	1/2 tsp.	2 mL
Pepper	1/4 tsp.	1 mL
Coarsely crushed tortilla chips	2 cups	500 mL
Grated Monterey Jack cheese	2 cups	500 mL
Sour cream, for garnish		
Salsa, for garnish		

Heat cooking oil in large frying pan on medium-high. Add ground beef and onion. Scramble-fry for 5 to 10 minutes until beef is no longer pink and onion is softened. Drain.

Add flour. Heat and stir for 1 minute. Add tomatoes. Heat and stir for about 1 minute, breaking up tomatoes with spoon, until mixture is boiling and thickened.

Add next 4 ingredients. Stir. Reduce heat to medium. Simmer, uncovered, for 4 minutes, stirring occasionally, to blend flavours.

Sprinkle tortilla chips and cheese over top. Broil 6 inches (15 cm) from heat in oven (see Note) for about 5 minutes until cheese is bubbling and golden. Let stand for 5 minutes. Cuts into 4 wedges.

Garnish individual servings with sour cream and salsa. Serves 4.

1 serving: 616 Calories; 36.3 g Total Fat (14.3 g Mono, 2.5 g Poly, 16.6 g Sat); 112 mg Cholesterol; 35 g Carbohydrate; 5 g Fibre; 40 g Protein; 1527 mg Sodium

Note: To avoid damaging frying pan handle in oven, wrap handle with foil before placing under broiler.

Make It A Meal with a salad of mixed greens, sliced ripe olives, chopped green onion and diced avocado drizzled with a herb and tomato dressing.

Grilled Steak And Onions

Sun-dried tomato pesto and balsamic vinegar add interest
to simple steak and onions. Very tasty.

Cooking oil	1 tbsp.	15 mL
Thinly sliced onion	2 cups	500 mL
Garlic cloves, minced (or 1/2 tsp., 2 mL, powder)	2	2
Strip loin steak, cut into 4 equal portions	1 lb.	454 g
Parsley flakes, sprinkle		
Salt, sprinkle		
Pepper, sprinkle		
Sun-dried tomato pesto	2 tbsp.	30 mL
Balsamic vinegar	1 1/2 tbsp.	25 mL
Brown sugar, packed	1 tsp.	5 mL

Preheat electric grill for 5 minutes or gas barbecue to medium-high (see Note). Heat cooking oil in large frying pan on medium. Add onion and garlic. Cook for 5 to 10 minutes, stirring often, until onion is softened. Set aside.

Sprinkle both sides of each steak portion with parsley, salt and pepper. Cook on greased grill for about 4 minutes per side until desired doneness. Transfer to large plate. Cover with foil. Let stand for 5 minutes.

Add pesto, vinegar and brown sugar to onion mixture. Heat and stir on medium for about 1 minute until heated through. Place 1 steak portion on each of 4 plates. Spoon onion mixture onto steak. Serves 4.

1 serving: 341 Calories; 22.5 g Total Fat (10.4 g Mono, 1.8 g Poly, 7.9 g Sat); 60 mg Cholesterol; 10 g Carbohydrate; 1 g Fibre; 24 g Protein; 70 mg Sodium

Note: Steak may be broiled in oven. Place on greased broiler pan. Broil about 4 inches (10 cm) from heat in oven for about 4 minutes per side until desired doneness.

Make It A Meal with microwaved "baked" potatoes (with skin) loaded with your favourite condiments. Serve with a mixture of steamed sugar snap peas and sliced carrots dotted with margarine or butter and sprinkled with toasted sesame seeds.

Asian Beef Wraps

Asian flavours wrapped in tortillas. Delightfully different.

Water	1 cup	250 mL
Long grain white rice	1/2 cup	125 mL
Salt	1/2 tsp.	2 mL
Cooking oil	1 tbsp.	15 mL
Beef top sirloin steak, cut diagonally across grain into 1/8 inch (3 mm) slices (see Tip, page 13)	1 lb.	454 g
Teriyaki sauce	1/2 cup	125 mL
Bag of broccoli slaw (or shredded cabbage with carrot)	12 oz.	340 g
Thinly sliced green pepper	1/2 cup	125 mL
Sliced green onion	2 tbsp.	30 mL
Minced pickled ginger slices, drained	1 tbsp.	15 mL
Garlic clove, minced (or 1/4 tsp., 1 mL, powder)	1	1
Flour tortillas (9 inch, 22 cm, diameter)	8	8

Combine water, rice and salt in small saucepan. Stir. Bring to a boil on high. Reduce heat to medium-low. Cover. Simmer for about 15 minutes, without stirring, until rice is tender. Remove from heat. Fluff rice with fork. Cover to keep warm.

Meanwhile, heat wok or large frying pan on medium-high until very hot. Add cooking oil. Add beef. Stir-fry for about 4 minutes until desired doneness.

Add teriyaki sauce. Stir until beef is coated. Transfer to medium bowl. Cover to keep warm.

Stir-fry next 5 ingredients in same wok for about 3 minutes until vegetables are tender-crisp. Add beef and rice. Heat and stir for about 1 minute until heated through.

(continued on next page)

Beef

Sprinkle 1 side of each tortilla with a few drops of water. Stack on large microwave-safe plate. Cover. Microwave on medium (50%) for 1 to 2 minutes until warm. Spoon beef mixture across centre of each tortilla. Fold sides over filling. Roll up from bottom to enclose. Makes 8 wraps.

1 wrap: 309 Calories; 9.8 g Total Fat (4.3 g Mono, 1.9 g Poly, 2.6 g Sat); 28 mg Cholesterol; 37 g Carbohydrate; 3 g Fibre; 18 g Protein; 1105 mg Sodium

Make It A Meal with a salad of torn romaine lettuce, fresh snow peas, slivers of red pepper and sliced green onion tossed with a ginger dressing.

ASIAN BEEF RICE BOWLS: Omit water, rice, salt and tortillas. Cook 1 1/2 cups (375 mL) long grain white rice according to package directions. Fluff with fork. Spoon into individual bowls. Top with beef mixture.

Paré Pointer
Mr. and Mrs. Grape went their separate ways.
They were tired of raisin kids.

Hurry Chimichurri Patties

Chimichurri is a thick herb sauce that's as common in Argentina as ketchup is in North America. Lots of fresh herb flavour in these zesty patties.

Large egg	1	1
Cornflake crumbs	1/3 cup	75 mL
Fine dry bread crumbs	1/3 cup	75 mL
Medium salsa	1/3 cup	75 mL
Basil pesto	2 tbsp.	30 mL
Lean ground turkey	1 lb.	454 g
Cooking oil	1 tsp.	5 mL
CHIMICHURRI SAUCE		
Fresh parsley, lightly packed	1 cup	250 mL
Olive (or cooking) oil	3 tbsp.	50 mL
Fresh oregano leaves	2 tbsp.	30 mL
Balsamic vinegar	1 tbsp.	15 mL
Garlic clove, minced (or 1/4 tsp., 1 mL, powder)	1	1
Dried crushed chilies	1/2 tsp.	2 mL

Beat egg with fork in large bowl. Add next 4 ingredients. Stir well. Add ground turkey. Mix well. Divide and shape into four 5 to 6 inch (12.5 to 15 cm) diameter patties.

Heat cooking oil in large frying pan on medium. Add patties. Cook for about 7 minutes per side until no longer pink inside. Meanwhile, prepare Chimichurri Sauce.

Chimichurri Sauce: Process all 6 ingredients in blender or food processor until paste-like consistency. Makes about 1/2 cup (125 mL) sauce. Serve with patties. Serves 4.

1 serving: 420 Calories; 26.6 g Total Fat (14.7 g Mono, 4.5 g Poly, 5.1 g Sat); 138 mg Cholesterol; 18 g Carbohydrate; 1 g Fibre; 27 g Protein; 338 mg Sodium

Pictured on page 35.

Make It A Meal with frozen potato pieces (such as tater tots) cooked according to package directions. Serve patties in a Kaiser roll with lettuce, tomato and your favourite condiments. Add some steamed mixed veggies on the side.

Mediterranean Chicken

An attractive, colourful dish you'll want to make often.

Cooking oil	1 tbsp.	15 mL
Boneless, skinless chicken breast halves, chopped	1 1/4 lbs.	560 g
Sliced fresh white mushrooms	2 cups	500 mL
Sliced red pepper	1 cup	250 mL
Dried basil (or 2 tbsp., 30 mL, finely shredded fresh)	1 1/2 tsp.	7 mL
Garlic powder	1/2 tsp.	2 mL
Salt	1/4 tsp.	1 mL
Pepper	1/4 tsp.	1 mL
Fresh spinach leaves, lightly packed	3 cups	750 mL
Grated Parmesan cheese	1/4 cup	60 mL
Lemon juice	1 tbsp.	15 mL

Heat cooking oil in large frying pan on medium-high. Add chicken. Cook for about 5 minutes, stirring occasionally, until no longer pink inside.

Add next 6 ingredients. Heat and stir for about 5 minutes until red pepper is softened.

Add spinach. Heat and stir for 1 to 2 minutes until spinach starts to wilt.

Add Parmesan cheese and lemon juice. Stir well. Serves 4.

1 serving: 250 Calories; 8.2 g Total Fat (3.2 g Mono, 1.8 g Poly, 2.2 g Sat); 86 mg Cholesterol; 7 g Carbohydrate; 2 g Fibre; 37 g Protein; 310 mg Sodium

Make It A Meal with couscous cooked in chicken broth and a spoonful of tomato pesto.

Paré Pointer

The one who was most thirsty drank Canada Dry.

Quesadillas Olé

A creative combination of ingredients makes these
spicy chicken quesadillas just the ticket for dinner.

Cooking oil	1 tsp.	5 mL
Lean ground chicken	1 lb.	454 g
Chopped onion	1/2 cup	125 mL
Garlic clove, minced (or 1/4 tsp., 1 mL, powder)	1	1
Frozen kernel corn, thawed	1 cup	250 mL
Medium salsa	1 cup	250 mL
Chili paste (sambal oelek)	1 tsp.	5 mL
Chili powder	1 tsp.	5 mL
Ground cumin	1 tsp.	5 mL
Grated Monterey Jack With Jalapeño cheese	1 cup	250 mL
Sun-dried tomato (or plain) flour tortillas (9 inch, 22 cm, diameter)	4	4
Hard margarine (or butter)	2 tsp.	10 mL

Heat cooking oil in large frying pan on medium-high. Add ground chicken. Scramble-fry for 5 to 10 minutes until no longer pink. Drain.

Add onion and garlic. Heat and stir for 2 to 3 minutes until onion starts to soften.

Add next 5 ingredients. Heat and stir for 2 to 3 minutes until liquid is evaporated and onion is softened.

Sprinkle 2 tbsp. (30 mL) cheese over half of each tortilla, almost to edge. Scatter chicken mixture over cheese on each. Sprinkle with remaining cheese. Fold unfilled tortilla halves over cheese. Press down lightly.

Melt 1 tsp. (5 mL) margarine in same large frying pan on medium. Carefully place 2 folded tortillas in pan. Cook for about 2 minutes until bottom of each quesadilla is golden and brown spots appear. Carefully turn quesadillas over. Cook for about 2 minutes until golden and cheese is melted. Repeat with remaining margarine and folded tortillas. Makes 4 quesadillas.

(continued on next page)

1 quesadilla: 552 Calories; 30.9 g Total Fat (5.8 g Mono, 2.1 g Poly, 6.7 g Sat); 27 mg Cholesterol; 37 g Carbohydrate; 4 g Fibre; 33 g Protein; 624 mg Sodium

Make It A Meal with a spicy, heat-and-serve tomato and herb soup. Stir in a spoonful of sour cream or yogurt for a milder taste.

Sweet Orange Chicken

Tender chicken and carrot smothered in a sweet and spicy glaze will have them asking for more!

Water	1 tbsp.	15 mL
Cornstarch	2 tsp.	10 mL
Cooking oil	1 tsp.	5 mL
Boneless, skinless chicken thighs, quartered	1 lb.	454 g
Thinly sliced carrot	3/4 cup	175 mL
Orange juice	3/4 cup	175 mL
Brown sugar, packed	1 tbsp.	15 mL
Balsamic vinegar	2 tsp.	10 mL
Hoisin sauce	2 tsp.	10 mL
Salt	1/8 tsp.	0.5 mL
Pepper	1/4 tsp.	1 mL

Stir water into cornstarch in small cup until smooth. Set aside.

Heat cooking oil in large frying pan on medium-high. Add chicken. Cook for about 5 minutes, stirring occasionally, until browned.

Combine remaining 7 ingredients in small bowl. Add to chicken. Stir. Bring to a boil. Reduce heat to medium-low. Cover. Simmer for about 6 minutes until chicken is no longer pink inside and carrot is tender-crisp. Stir cornstarch mixture. Add to chicken mixture. Heat and stir for about 1 minute until sauce is boiling and thickened. Serves 4.

1 serving: 223 Calories; 7.5 g Total Fat (2.6 g Mono, 1.9 g Poly, 1.7 g Sat); 94 mg Cholesterol; 16 g Carbohydrate; 1 g Fibre; 23 g Protein; 198 mg Sodium

Make It A Meal with couscous and frozen peas cooked together in chicken or vegetable broth. Sprinkle with toasted sesame seeds before serving.

Spicy Chicken And Salsa

Heat things up tonight with flavourful, spicy chicken.
Cooling Cucumber Salsa helps tame the flame!

Olive (or cooking) oil	2 tsp.	10 mL
Curry powder	2 tsp.	10 mL
Chili powder	1 tsp.	5 mL
Brown sugar, packed	1 tsp.	5 mL
Ground allspice	1/8 tsp.	0.5 mL
Salt	1/4 tsp.	1 mL
Pepper	1/4 tsp.	1 mL
Boneless, skinless chicken breast halves (4 – 6 oz., 113 – 170 g, each)	4	4
CUCUMBER SALSA		
Chopped English cucumber (with peel)	1 cup	250 mL
Plain yogurt	1/3 cup	75 mL
Finely chopped red onion	1/4 cup	60 mL
Garlic clove, minced (or 1/4 tsp., 1 mL, powder)	1	1
Lime (or lemon) juice	1 tsp.	5 mL
Salt, sprinkle		
Pepper, sprinkle		

Preheat electric grill for 5 minutes or gas barbecue to medium (see Note). Measure first 7 ingredients into small cup. Stir until paste-like consistency.

Rub curry mixture on both sides of each chicken breast half. Cook on greased grill for about 5 minutes per side until no longer pink inside. Meanwhile prepare Cucumber Salsa.

Cucumber Salsa: Combine all 7 ingredients in small bowl. Makes about 1 cup (250 mL) salsa. Serve with chicken. Serves 4.

1 serving: 209 Calories; 5.3 g Total Fat (2.4 g Mono, 0.8 g Poly, 1.2 g Sat); 83 mg Cholesterol; 6 g Carbohydrate; 1 g Fibre; 33 g Protein; 172 mg Sodium

Pictured on front cover.

Note: Chicken may be broiled in oven. Place on greased broiler pan. Broil about 4 inches (10 cm) from heat in oven for about 5 minutes per side until no longer pink inside.

(continued on next page)

Make It A Meal with baby potatoes cooked in microwave until tender, dotted with margarine or butter and sprinkled with dill, salt and pepper.

Springtime Chicken Pizza

This cheesy chicken pizza, topped with lots of veggies,
is destined to become a year-round favourite.

Prebaked pizza crust (12 inch, 30 cm, diameter)	1	1
Pizza sauce	1/3 cup	75 mL
Grated Parmesan cheese	1/2 cup	125 mL
Chopped cooked chicken	1 1/2 cups	375 mL
Roasted red peppers, drained, blotted dry, cut into strips	1/3 cup	75 mL
Fresh asparagus spears, trimmed of tough ends	8	8
Goat (chèvre) cheese, cut up	2/3 cup	150 mL

Preheat oven to 475°F (240°C). Place pizza crust on greased 12 inch (30 cm) pizza pan. Spread pizza sauce evenly on crust. Sprinkle with Parmesan cheese.

Scatter chicken and red pepper over Parmesan cheese.

Arrange asparagus spears in spoke pattern on top of red pepper. Scatter goat cheese over top. Bake for about 15 minutes until crust is crisp and golden. Cuts into 8 wedges.

1 wedge: 246 Calories; 10.5 g Total Fat (2.7 g Mono, 0.8 g Poly, 5.2 g Sat); 43 mg Cholesterol; 19 g Carbohydrate; 1 g Fibre; 18 g Protein; 455 mg Sodium

Pictured on page 36.

Make It A Meal with a salad of lettuce, grated carrot and sliced tomato drizzled with a roasted red pepper dressing.

Crumby Chicken Strips

Serve these golden-crumbed chicken strips with
plum or honey mustard dipping sauce.

Large eggs	**2**	**2**
Cornflake crumbs	**1 cup**	**250 mL**
Grated Parmesan cheese	**1/2 cup**	**125 mL**
Lemon pepper	**1 tbsp.**	**15 mL**
Chicken breast cutlets (about 1 lb., **454 g), each cut into 3 equal pieces**	**4**	**4**

Preheat oven to 425°F (220°C). Beat eggs with fork in small shallow dish.

Combine next 3 ingredients in shallow medium dish.

Dip each chicken piece in egg. Press both sides of each piece into crumb mixture until coated. Place on greased baking sheet with sides. Spray top of chicken pieces with cooking spray. Bake for about 15 minutes until no longer pink inside. Makes 12 chicken strips. Serves 4.

1 serving: 322 Calories; 8.5 g Total Fat (2.6 g Mono, 0.9 g Poly, 3.8 g Sat); 184 mg Cholesterol; 23 g Carbohydrate; 1 g Fibre; 36 g Protein; 966 mg Sodium

Pictured on page 35.

Make It A Meal with frozen potato pieces (tater tots, gems or puffs) cooked according to package directions and sprinkled with Cajun spices and pepper.

1. Crumby Chicken Strips, above
2. Hurry Chimichurri Patties, page 28

Chicken & Poultry

Pecan-Crusted Chicken

Seasoned with honey mustard and coated with pecans,
this easy-to-make chicken is special enough for company.

Dijon mustard	3 tbsp.	50 mL
Liquid honey	2 tbsp.	30 mL
Boneless, skinless chicken breast halves (4 – 6 oz., 113 – 170 g, each)	4	4
Ground pecans	3/4 cup	175 mL
Fine dry bread crumbs	1/4 cup	60 mL
Hard margarine (or butter), melted	2 tbsp.	30 mL
Dried basil	1 tsp.	5 mL
Salt	1/4 tsp.	1 mL

Preheat oven to 425°F (220°C). Combine mustard and honey in small bowl. Brush on both sides of each chicken breast half.

Combine remaining 5 ingredients in medium shallow dish. Press both sides of each chicken breast half into crumb mixture until coated. Place on greased baking sheet with sides. Bake for 15 to 20 minutes until chicken is no longer pink inside and crumb mixture is golden. Serves 4.

1 serving: 399 Calories; 21.9 g Total Fat (12.5 g Mono, 4.8 g Poly, 3 g Sat); 77 mg Cholesterol; 18 g Carbohydrate; 2 g Fibre; 34 g Protein; 510 mg Sodium

Make It A Meal with a salad of fresh spinach leaves, sliced mushrooms and croutons tossed with ranch-style dressing. Or try cooked sliced carrots glazed with a mixture of margarine or butter and a little honey.

1. Pesto Pizza, page 19
2. Peppy Personal Pizzas, page 88
3. Springtime Chicken Pizza, page 33

Props courtesy of: Danesco Inc.

Southwestern Spuds

How does something so simple taste so good? Easy!

Large potatoes (with skin)	4	4
Cooking oil	2 tsp.	10 mL
Sliced fresh white mushrooms	1 cup	250 mL
Chopped green pepper	1/2 cup	125 mL
Chopped cooked chicken	2 cups	500 mL
Medium salsa	1 cup	250 mL
Sour cream	1 cup	250 mL
Grated medium Cheddar cheese	1/2 cup	125 mL

Poke several holes randomly with fork in each potato. Wrap each with paper towel. Microwave on high (100%) for about 15 minutes, turning potatoes over at halftime, until tender.

Meanwhile, heat cooking oil in large frying pan on medium-high. Add mushrooms and green pepper. Cook for about 2 minutes, stirring occasionally, until vegetables start to soften.

Add chicken and salsa. Heat and stir for about 3 minutes until heated through. Reduce heat to medium-low.

Add sour cream. Stir well. Remove from heat. Cover to keep warm. Cut potatoes in half lengthwise. Without damaging skin, carefully mash inside of each potato with fork. Place 2 potato halves on each of 4 plates. Spoon chicken mixture onto each potato half.

Sprinkle cheese over top. Serves 4.

1 serving: 473 Calories; 21.8 g Total Fat (7.2 g Mono, 2.6 g Poly, 10.2 g Sat); 106 mg Cholesterol; 38 g Carbohydrate; 5 g Fibre; 33 g Protein; 374 mg Sodium

Make It A Meal with a salsa made with chopped tomato, diced avocado, chopped fresh cilantro and diced red onion. Combine 2 tbsp. (30 mL) lime juice, 1 tbsp. (15 mL) olive oil and a sprinkle each of salt and pepper in small cup. Drizzle over vegetables and toss to coat.

Chicken & Poultry

Folded Sombreros

Tasty quesadillas filled with loads of Southwestern flavour are baked to perfection. A family-friendly meal.

Flour tortillas (9 inch, 22 cm, diameter)	4	4
Salsa	1/2 cup	125 mL
Cooking oil	1 tsp.	5 mL
Lean ground turkey	1 lb.	454 g
Lemon pepper	2 tsp.	10 mL
Garlic clove, minced (or 1/4 tsp., 1 mL, powder)	1	1
Thinly sliced red onion	1/2 cup	125 mL
Chopped fresh cilantro or parsley	3 tbsp.	50 mL
Pickled pepper rings	1/4 cup	60 mL
Ripe large avocado, sliced	1	1
Grated Monterey Jack cheese	1 1/3 cups	325 mL

Preheat oven to 425°F (220°C). Place tortillas on 2 greased baking sheets. Spread salsa evenly on each tortilla, almost to edge.

Heat cooking oil in large frying pan on medium-high. Add ground turkey, lemon pepper and garlic. Scramble-fry for 5 to 10 minutes until turkey is no longer pink. Drain. Scatter on half of each tortilla.

Divide and layer next 5 ingredients, in order given, on top of turkey mixture on each. Fold unfilled tortilla halves over cheese. Press down lightly. Bake on separate racks in oven for about 15 minutes, switching position of baking sheets at halftime, until cheese is melted and edges start to brown. Makes 4 quesadillas.

1 quesadilla: 597 Calories; 36.2 g Total Fat (15.1 g Mono, 5.7 g Poly, 12.4 g Sat); 120 mg Cholesterol; 31 g Carbohydrate; 4 g Fibre; 38 g Protein; 986 mg Sodium

Make It A Meal with a salad of coleslaw mix, diced red pepper and kernel corn drizzled with a herb vinaigrette.

Paré Pointer

A sure sign of age is when snap, crackle and pop are not just a cereal.

Poached Lemon Chicken

*Lemon and white wine sauce gently infused with rosemary
adds sophisticated flavour to tender chicken.*

Water	1 tbsp.	15 mL
Cornstarch	1 tbsp.	15 mL
Parsley flakes	1 1/2 tsp.	7 mL
Prepared chicken broth	1 1/2 cups	375 mL
Dry white (or alcohol-free) wine	1/2 cup	125 mL
Sprigs of fresh rosemary	2	2
Boneless, skinless chicken breast halves (4 – 6 oz., 113 – 170 g, each)	4	4
Lemon pepper	1 tsp.	5 mL
Thin lemon slices	12	12

Stir water into cornstarch and parsley in small cup. Set aside.

Measure broth and wine into medium frying pan. Stir. Add rosemary sprigs.

Place chicken breast halves in wine mixture. Sprinkle with lemon pepper. Place 3 lemon slices on each chicken breast half. Bring to a boil on medium-high. Reduce heat to medium-low. Cover. Simmer for 10 to 15 minutes until chicken is no longer pink inside. Discard lemon slices and rosemary sprigs. Remove chicken with slotted spoon to large serving dish. Cover to keep warm. Increase heat to medium-high. Stir cornstarch mixture. Add to broth mixture. Heat and stir for about 1 minute until boiling and thickened. Remove to small serving bowl. Serve with chicken. Serves 4.

1 serving: 194 Calories; 2.7 g Total Fat (0.8 g Mono, 0.6 g Poly, 0.7 g Sat); 77 mg Cholesterol; 3 g Carbohydrate; trace Fibre; 32 g Protein; 532 mg Sodium

Make It A Meal with hot buttered egg noodles tossed with onion salt and a small spoonful of poppy seeds. Sauté mushrooms and add to noodles, if desired.

Chicken And Greens

Spicy peanut sauce coats tender-crisp veggies and chicken.
A sprinkling of peanuts adds the perfect punch.

Peanut sauce	2 tbsp.	30 mL
Oyster sauce	2 tbsp.	30 mL
Low-sodium soy sauce	1 1/2 tbsp.	25 mL
Cornstarch	1 tbsp.	15 mL
Cooking oil	2 tbsp.	30 mL
Boneless, skinless chicken breast halves, cut across grain into thin slices (see Tip, page 13)	1 lb.	454 g
Shredded suey choy (Chinese cabbage)	4 cups	1 L
Chopped bok choy	4 cups	1 L
Chopped unsalted peanuts	2 tbsp.	30 mL

Combine first 4 ingredients in small bowl. Set aside.

Heat wok or large frying pan on medium-high until very hot. Add cooking oil. Add chicken. Stir-fry for 3 to 5 minutes until no longer pink.

Add suey choy and bok choy. Stir-fry for about 2 minutes until tender-crisp. Stir cornstarch mixture. Add to chicken mixture. Heat and stir for about 1 minute until sauce is boiling and thickened. Remove to large serving dish.

Sprinkle with peanuts. Serves 4.

1 serving: 293 Calories; 13.5 g Total Fat (6.5 g Mono, 3.8 g Poly, 2.1 g Sat); 66 mg Cholesterol; 14 g Carbohydrate; 2 g Fibre; 30 g Protein; 592 mg Sodium

Make It A Meal with Chinese egg noodles cooked according to package directions, then fried in a little peanut oil until just brown and crisp.

Paré Pointer
If only we could get an ambulance as fast as pizza delivery.

Thai Fish Cakes

Lime and ginger add a subtle accent to tender fish cakes.

Chopped red pepper	1/2 cup	125 mL
Large egg	1	1
Green onions, coarsely chopped	2	2
Fish sauce	2 tbsp.	30 mL
Chili paste (sambal oelek)	1 tbsp.	15 mL
Coarsely chopped, peeled gingerroot	1 tbsp.	15 mL
Lime juice	2 tsp.	10 mL
Garlic clove, coarsely chopped (or 1/4 tsp., 1 mL, powder)	1	1
Grated lime zest	1/2 tsp.	2 mL
Skinless white fish fillets (such as cod, sole or bluefish), blotted dry, any small bones removed, cut up	14 oz.	395 g
Fine dry bread crumbs	2 tbsp.	30 mL
Fine dry bread crumbs	1/2 cup	125 mL
Cooking oil	3 tbsp.	50 mL

Put first 9 ingredients into food processor. Pulse with on/off motion, scraping down side if necessary, until almost smooth.

Add fish and first amount of bread crumbs. Pulse with on/off motion until fish is finely chopped. Shape mixture into 8 patties, using 1/3 cup (75 mL) for each.

Press both sides of each patty into second amount of bread crumbs in small shallow dish until coated.

Heat cooking oil in large frying pan on medium-high. Add patties. Cook for 3 to 5 minutes per side until golden and fish is firm. Transfer to paper towels to drain. Makes 8 fish cakes.

1 fish cake: 164 Calories; 9.2 g Total Fat (4.5 g Mono, 2.8 g Poly, 1.1 g Sat); 57 mg Cholesterol; 8 g Carbohydrate; 1 g Fibre; 12 g Protein; 371 mg Sodium

Make It A Meal with thinly sliced English cucumber drizzled with a dressing of plain yogurt and dill weed. Sprinkle with salt, pepper and toasted sesame seeds before serving.

Quickest Cioppino

Cioppino (chuh-PEE-noh) is a zesty tomato-based seafood stew.
Fragrant basil and oregano add just the right touch.

Can of diced tomatoes (with juice)	14 oz.	398 mL
Can of tomato sauce	14 oz.	398 mL
Chopped potato (with skin)	1 cup	250 mL
Medium salsa	1 cup	250 mL
Garlic powder	1/2 tsp.	2 mL
Dried basil	1/2 tsp.	2 mL
Dried whole oregano	1/4 tsp.	1 mL
Dried thyme	1/4 tsp.	1 mL
Can of whole baby clams (with liquid)	5 oz.	142 g
Frozen uncooked medium shrimp (peeled, deveined), thawed	1/2 lb.	225 g
Skinless firm white fish fillets (such as cod or halibut), any small bones removed, cut into 1 inch (2.5 cm) pieces	1/2 lb.	225 g

Combine first 8 ingredients in large pot or Dutch oven. Bring to a boil on high. Reduce heat to medium-low. Cover. Simmer for about 10 minutes until potato is tender.

Add remaining 3 ingredients. Stir. Cover. Cook on medium-high for about 3 minutes until shrimp turn pink and fish flakes easily when tested with fork. Serves 6.

1 serving: 176 Calories; 3.6 g Total Fat (0.9 g Mono, 1.3 g Poly, 0.6 g Sat); 90 mg Cholesterol; 16 g Carbohydrate; 3 g Fibre; 21 g Protein; 790 mg Sodium

Pictured on page 143 and on back cover.

Make It A Meal with fresh multi-grain bread or heat-and-serve garlic bread.

Paré Pointer

His business is to invest all your money. He's a broker.

Curry In A Hurry

A quick, colourful stir-fry with enough sauce to serve over rice.
Mild curry adds a pleasing heat.

Cooking oil	1 tbsp.	15 mL
Chopped red onion	3/4 cup	175 mL
Garlic cloves, minced (or 1 tsp., 5 mL, powder)	4	4
Mild curry paste	2 tbsp.	30 mL
Chopped peeled yam (or sweet potato)	1 1/2 cups	375 mL
Can of coconut milk	14 oz.	398 mL
Prepared chicken broth	1/2 cup	125 mL
Fresh (or frozen, thawed) green beans, cut into 2 inch (5 cm) pieces	1 1/2 cups	375 mL
Frozen uncooked large shrimp (peeled, deveined), thawed	1 lb.	454 g
Salted cashews (or peanuts)	1/3 cup	75 mL

Heat wok or large frying pan on medium-high until very hot. Add cooking oil. Add onion, garlic and curry paste. Heat and stir for about 1 minute until fragrant.

Add yam, coconut milk and broth. Stir. Bring to a boil. Boil, uncovered, for 8 to 10 minutes, stirring occasionally, until yam is tender.

Add beans. Stir. Cook, uncovered, for 3 to 5 minutes, stirring occasionally, until beans are tender-crisp.

Add shrimp. Stir. Cook, uncovered, for about 3 minutes, without stirring, until shrimp turn pink.

Add cashews. Stir. Serves 4.

1 serving: 505 Calories; 33.9 g Total Fat (7.8 g Mono, 3.6 g Poly, 19.9 g Sat); 129 mg Cholesterol; 31 g Carbohydrate; 4 g Fibre; 24 g Protein; 253 mg Sodium

Pictured on page 53.

Make It A Meal with hot basmati rice. Serve with sliced tomatoes and English cucumber on the side.

Salmon With Mango Sauce

Creamy mango sauce is the perfect partner to tender, pan-fried salmon.

Lime juice	3 tbsp.	50 mL
Sweet chili sauce	3 tbsp.	50 mL
Fresh (or frozen, thawed) salmon fillets (about 1 lb., 454 g), skin removed	4	4
Salt, sprinkle		
Pepper, sprinkle		
Cooking oil	1 tbsp.	15 mL
MANGO SAUCE		
Can of sliced mango in syrup (14 oz., 398 mL), drained and juice reserved (see Note)	1/2	1/2
Plain yogurt	1/4 cup	60 mL
Lime juice	1 1/2 tsp.	7 mL
Sweet chili sauce	1 1/2 tsp.	7 mL
Dried cilantro or parsley flakes	3/4 tsp.	4 mL
Salt	1/8 tsp.	0.5 mL

Combine lime juice and chili sauce in small cup. Brush on both sides of each salmon fillet. Sprinkle each side with salt and pepper.

Heat cooking oil in large frying pan on medium. Add fillets. Cook for about 5 minutes per side until fish flakes easily when tested with fork. Meanwhile, prepare Mango Sauce.

Mango Sauce: Process all 6 ingredients in blender or food processor until smooth. Makes about 1 cup (250 mL) sauce. Serve with salmon fillets. Serves 4.

1 serving: 244 Calories; 11.1 g Total Fat (4.5 g Mono, 3.9 g Poly, 1.6 g Sat); 63 mg Cholesterol; 12 g Carbohydrate; 2 g Fibre; 24 g Protein; 342 mg Sodium

Pictured on page 53.

Note: Use mango juice to cook rice or use in your favourite dessert recipe.

Make It A Meal with long grain rice cooked in juice drained from mango plus additional water. Dice remaining mango and stir into cooked rice along with toasted slivered almonds.

Spud-Crusted Haddock

These attractive, potato-crusted fish fillets are sure to be a hit.

Hard margarine (or butter), melted	1/4 cup	60 mL
Instant potato flakes	2/3 cup	150 mL
Lemon pepper	1/2 tsp.	2 mL
Onion powder	1/4 tsp.	1 mL
Seasoned salt	1/8 tsp.	0.5 mL
Haddock fillets (about 1 lb., 454 g), blotted dry	4	4

Preheat oven to 400°F (205°C). Pour margarine into shallow medium dish.

Combine next 4 ingredients in separate shallow medium dish.

Dip each fillet in margarine. Press both sides of each fillet into potato flake mixture until coated. Arrange in single layer in greased 9 × 13 inch (22 × 33 cm) pan. Sprinkle any excess potato flake mixture over fillets. Drizzle any excess melted margarine over top. Bake for about 15 minutes until potato mixture is golden and fish flakes easily when tested with fork. Serves 4.

1 serving: 236 Calories; 13 g Total Fat (8.1 g Mono, 1.5 g Poly, 2.7 g Sat); 65 mg Cholesterol; 7 g Carbohydrate; 1 g Fibre; 22 g Protein; 300 mg Sodium

Make It A Meal with sliced tomatoes sprinkled with salt and freshly ground pepper. Serve with steamed asparagus spears drizzled with a vinaigrette dressing.

 To toast nuts, seeds or coconut, spread evenly in ungreased shallow pan. Bake in 350°F (175°C) oven for 5 to 10 minutes, stirring or shaking often, until desired doneness.

Broccoli Shrimp Stir-Fry

The secret to a great stir-fry? Flavours that remain in your memory!

Prepared chicken broth	3/4 cup	175 mL
Hoisin sauce	2 tbsp.	30 mL
Cornstarch	2 tsp.	10 mL
Chinese five-spice powder	1/8 tsp.	0.5 mL
Pepper	1/8 tsp.	0.5 mL
Cooking oil	1 tsp.	5 mL
Frozen uncooked medium shrimp (peeled, deveined), thawed	1 lb.	454 g
Cooking oil	2 tsp.	10 mL
Broccoli florets	3 cups	750 mL
Chopped green onion	1/2 cup	125 mL
Toasted slivered almonds (see Tip, page 46)	1/4 cup	60 mL

Combine first 5 ingredients in small bowl. Set aside.

Heat wok or large frying pan on medium-high until very hot. Add first amount of cooking oil. Add shrimp. Stir-fry for about 1 minute until shrimp just turn pink. Transfer to medium bowl.

Heat second amount of cooking oil in same wok. Add broccoli and green onion. Stir-fry for 1 minute. Stir cornstarch mixture. Add to vegetables. Heat and stir for about 3 minutes until sauce is boiling and thickened and broccoli is tender-crisp.

Add shrimp and almonds. Stir-fry for about 1 minute until shrimp are heated through. Serves 4.

1 serving: 227 Calories; 10 g Total Fat (5.3 g Mono, 2.8 g Poly, 1.1 g Sat); 129 mg Cholesterol; 14 g Carbohydrate; 3 g Fibre; 22 g Protein; 644 mg Sodium

Pictured on page 90.

Make It A Meal with long grain rice. Add 1 1/2 cups (375 mL) frozen peas to rice during last 5 minutes of cooking time.

Ginger Lime Salmon Patties

Ginger and lime add light, refreshing flavour to delicate salmon patties.

Fresh salmon fillets, skin and any small bones removed, cut up	1 lb.	454 g
Fine dry bread crumbs	1/2 cup	125 mL
Thinly sliced green onion	1/4 cup	60 mL
Large egg	1	1
Grated lime zest	2 tsp.	10 mL
Soy sauce	2 tsp.	10 mL
Finely grated, peeled gingerroot	1 tsp.	5 mL
Salt	1/8 tsp.	0.5 mL
LIME SAUCE		
Mayonnaise (not salad dressing)	1/2 cup	125 mL
Toasted sesame seeds (see Tip, page 46)	2 tbsp.	30 mL
Lime juice	1 tbsp.	15 mL
Sweet chili sauce	1 tbsp.	15 mL
Cooking oil	1 tbsp.	15 mL

Process first 8 ingredients in food processor until almost smooth. Shape mixture into 8 patties, using 1/4 cup (60 mL) for each. Place on large plastic wrap-lined plate. Cover. Freeze for 10 minutes. Meanwhile, prepare Lime Sauce.

Lime Sauce: Combine first 4 ingredients in small bowl. Makes about 1/3 cup (75 mL) sauce. Cover. Chill.

Heat cooking oil in large frying pan on medium. Add patties. Cook for 3 to 5 minutes per side until fish is firm and golden. Serve with Lime Sauce. Serves 8.

1 serving: 259 Calories; 19.2 g Total Fat (9.5 g Mono, 6.5 g Poly, 2.2 g Sat); 67 mg Cholesterol; 7 g Carbohydrate; 1 g Fibre; 14 g Protein; 326 mg Sodium

Make It A Meal with hot chow mein noodles tossed with a small amount of sesame oil. Serve with steamed baby bok choy.

Lemon Pepper Sole

Mildly spiced Jalapeño Sauce adds interest to fish lightly breaded with a zesty coating of pepper and Parmesan cheese.

Fine dry bread crumbs	3/4 cup	175 mL
Grated Parmesan cheese	1 tbsp.	15 mL
Lemon pepper	1 tbsp.	15 mL
Large egg	1	1
Milk	1 tbsp.	15 mL
Sole fillets (about 1 lb., 454 g)	4	4
JALAPEÑO SAUCE		
Mayonnaise	1/4 cup	60 mL
Sour cream	2 tbsp.	30 mL
Chopped pickled jalapeño pepper (see Tip, page 23)	1 tbsp.	15 mL
Lemon juice	1/2 tsp.	2 mL

Preheat oven to 400°F (205°C). Combine first 3 ingredients in shallow medium dish.

Beat egg and milk with fork in separate shallow medium dish.

Dip each sole fillet in egg mixture. Press both sides of each fillet into bread crumb mixture until coated. Arrange in single layer on greased baking sheet with sides. Bake for about 10 minutes until fish flakes easily when tested with fork. Meanwhile, prepare Jalapeño Sauce.

Jalapeño Sauce: Combine all 4 ingredients in small bowl. Makes about 1/2 cup (125 mL) sauce. Serve with sole fillets. Serves 4.

1 serving: 336 Calories; 17.1 g Total Fat (8.2 g Mono, 4.9 g Poly, 3.1 g Sat); 121 mg Cholesterol; 17 g Carbohydrate; 1 g Fibre; 27 g Protein; 672 mg Sodium

Make It A Meal with hot jasmine rice and steamed broccoli.

Snappy Tostadas

Crisp, crunchy tortillas topped with zesty coleslaw and tender fish offer
something a little different for dinner.

Ranch-style dressing	1/2 cup	125 mL
Ground ginger	1 tsp.	5 mL
Pepper	1 tsp.	5 mL
Skinless snapper fillets (about 1 lb., 454 g), any small bones removed	4	4
Flour tortillas (9 inch, 22 cm, diameter)	4	4
Coleslaw mix	2 1/2 cups	625 mL
Chopped red pepper	1 cup	250 mL
Chopped onion	1/2 cup	125 mL

Preheat oven to 350°F (175°C). Combine first 3 ingredients in small bowl. Put 1/2 of mixture into small shallow dish. Set remaining mixture aside.

Dip both sides of each snapper fillet in dressing mixture in shallow dish. Place on greased baking sheet with sides. Bake for about 10 minutes until fish flakes easily when tested with fork. Transfer to medium bowl. Coarsely flake fish with fork.

Spray both sides of each tortilla with cooking spray. Arrange on 2 ungreased baking sheets. Bake on separate racks in oven for about 10 minutes, switching position of baking sheets at halftime, until golden.

Meanwhile, combine remaining 3 ingredients in large bowl. Add reserved dressing mixture. Mix well. Spread evenly on each tortilla. Spoon flaked fish onto coleslaw mixture. Makes 4 tostadas.

1 tostada: 404 Calories; 16.1 g Total Fat (7.9 g Mono, 5.6 g Poly, 1.6 g Sat); 51 mg Cholesterol; 35 g Carbohydrate; 4 g Fibre; 28 g Protein; 497 mg Sodium

Make It A Meal with a mixed bean salad from your grocer's deli and corn on the cob.

Salmon And Parsley Pesto

Tangy pesto provides a delicious contrast to mild, steamed salmon.

Fresh (or frozen, thawed) salmon fillets (about 1 lb., 454 g), skin removed	4	4
PARSLEY PESTO		
Fresh parsley, lightly packed	1 cup	250 mL
Lemon juice	1/4 cup	60 mL
Olive (or cooking) oil	2 tbsp.	30 mL
Creamed horseradish	2 tbsp.	30 mL
Garlic cloves, peeled	3	3
Salt	1/2 tsp.	2 mL

Set each salmon fillet on separate sheet of parchment paper in large bamboo steamer, or on wire rack, set over rapidly boiling water in wok or Dutch oven. Cover. Cook for about 10 minutes, depending on thickness of fillets, adding more boiling water to wok if necessary, until fish flakes easily when tested with fork. Meanwhile, prepare Parsley Pesto.

Parsley Pesto: Process all 6 ingredients in blender or food processor until smooth. Makes about 2/3 cup (150 mL) pesto. Serve with salmon fillets. Serves 4.

1 serving: 238 Calories; 14.2 g Total Fat (7.5 g Mono, 3.5 g Poly, 2.1 g Sat); 62 mg Cholesterol; 4 g Carbohydrate; trace Fibre; 23 g Protein; 363 mg Sodium

Make It A Meal with sliced tomatoes and mozzarella cheese sprinkled with salt, pepper and chopped fresh basil. Drizzle with small amounts of olive oil and balsamic vinegar.

Paré Pointer

Their garage is full of stuff not nearly as valuable as the two cars that have to sit in their driveway.

Caped Cod

All dressed up with a savoury soufflé coat. "Cod" it get any better?

Cod fillets (about 1 lb., 454 g), blotted dry	4	4
Lemon pepper	1/2 tsp.	2 mL
Onion salt	1/4 tsp.	1 mL
Egg white (large)	1	1
Salad dressing (or mayonnaise)	1/4 cup	60 mL
Dill weed	1/2 tsp.	2 mL

Preheat oven to 425°F (220°C). Sprinkle lemon pepper and onion salt over each fillet. Arrange in single layer in greased 3 quart (3 L) shallow baking dish.

Beat egg white in medium bowl until stiff peaks form. Fold in salad dressing and dill weed. Spoon onto each fillet. Bake for about 10 minutes until topping is puffed and golden and fish flakes easily when tested with fork. Serves 4.

1 serving: 176 Calories; 8.4 g Total Fat (4.4 g Mono, 2.8 g Poly, 0.7 g Sat); 53 mg Cholesterol; 2 g Carbohydrate; 0 g Fibre; 21 g Protein; 286 mg Sodium

Make It A Meal with egg noodles. Add 1 1/2 cups (375 mL) frozen mixed vegetables to noodles during last 5 minutes of cooking time. Drain. Toss with margarine or butter, salt and pepper.

1. Salmon With Mango Sauce, page 45
2. Curry In A Hurry, page 44

Props courtesy of: Cherison Enterprises Inc.
Island Pottery Inc.
Pfaltzgraff Canada

Fish & Seafood

Orange Sesame Salmon

Tender salmon fillets, topped with a ginger and orange glaze,
are fancy enough for company, but easy to make anytime.

Frozen concentrated orange juice, thawed	3 tbsp.	50 mL
Soy sauce	2 tbsp.	30 mL
Minced pickled ginger slices, drained	1 tbsp.	15 mL
Brown sugar, packed	1 tbsp.	15 mL
Sesame oil, for flavour	1 tsp.	5 mL
Fresh (or frozen, thawed) salmon fillets (about 1 lb., 454 g), skin removed	4	4
Toasted sesame seeds (see Tip, page 46)	2 tsp.	10 mL

Preheat oven to 450°F (230°C). Combine first 5 ingredients in small bowl.

Arrange salmon fillets in single layer in greased 8 x 8 inch (20 x 20 cm) pan. Spoon orange juice mixture onto each. Bake for about 10 minutes until fish flakes easily when tested with fork. Remove to large serving dish. Drizzle with sauce from pan.

Sprinkle with sesame seeds. Serves 4.

1 serving: 222 Calories; 9.2 g Total Fat (3.1 g Mono, 3.7 g Poly, 1.4 g Sat); 62 mg Cholesterol; 10 g Carbohydrate; trace Fibre; 24 g Protein; 575 mg Sodium

Make It A Meal with hot rice sprinkled with chopped green onion. Serve with steamed snow peas sprinkled with toasted sesame seeds.

Chipotle Chili Tacos, page 22

Props courtesy of: Browne & Co.
Danesco Inc.
Island Pottery Inc.

Black Bean Shrimp Noodles

A colourful stir-fry with the noodles built right in! A treat for your taste buds.

Bag of chow mein noodles	10 1/2 oz.	300 g
Boiling water		
Black bean sauce (pourable)	1/2 cup	125 mL
Water	2 tbsp.	30 mL
Medium sherry	1 tbsp.	15 mL
Cornstarch	1 1/2 tsp.	7 mL
Granulated sugar	1 tsp.	5 mL
Cooking oil	2 tsp.	10 mL
Halved fresh white mushrooms	2 cups	500 mL
Fresh vegetable stir-fry mix	4 cups	1 L
Finely grated, peeled gingerroot	2 tsp.	10 mL
Frozen uncooked medium shrimp (peeled, deveined), thawed	1 lb.	454 g

Put noodles into large bowl. Pour boiling water over top until covered. Let stand for about 5 minutes until softened. Drain. Set aside.

Meanwhile, combine next 5 ingredients in cup. Set aside.

Heat wok or large frying pan on medium-high until very hot. Add cooking oil. Add mushrooms. Stir-fry for about 2 minutes until mushrooms start to brown.

Add stir-fry mix and ginger. Stir-fry for 2 to 3 minutes until vegetables are almost tender-crisp.

Add shrimp. Stir-fry for 2 to 3 minutes until shrimp turn pink. Stir cornstarch mixture. Add to shrimp mixture. Add noodles. Heat and stir for about 2 minutes until sauce is boiling and thickened. Serves 4.

1 serving: 352 Calories; 9.4 g Total Fat (3.6 g Mono, 3.3 g Poly, 1.2 g Sat); 197 mg Cholesterol; 35 g Carbohydrate; 6 g Fibre; 33 g Protein; 1458 mg Sodium

Make It A Meal with heat-and-serve spring rolls or egg rolls (available in your grocer's freezer) cooked according to package directions and served with a tangy sweet-and-sour or plum sauce for dipping.

Fish & Seafood

Lemon Snapper Skillet

A simple but flavourful combination of lemon-zested fish and vegetables.

Frozen kernel corn	1 cup	250 mL
Frozen peas	1 cup	250 mL
Thinly sliced green onion	1/2 cup	125 mL
Salt	1/4 tsp.	1 mL
Skinless snapper fillets (about 1 lb., 454 g)	4	4
Hard margarine (or butter), melted	2 tbsp.	30 mL
Grated lemon zest	1 tsp.	5 mL
Salt	1/4 tsp.	1 mL
Pepper	1/4 tsp.	1 mL
Prepared chicken broth	1/2 cup	125 mL

Combine first 4 ingredients in medium frying pan.

Place snapper fillets on sheet of waxed paper on work surface. Brush margarine on top of each fillet. Sprinkle with lemon zest, salt and pepper. Fold fillets in half. Place on top of vegetable mixture in frying pan.

Add broth. Bring to a boil on high. Reduce heat to medium-low. Cover. Simmer for about 10 minutes until fish flakes easily when tested with fork. Remove fillets and vegetables with slotted spoon to large serving dish. Serves 4.

1 serving: 243 Calories; 8 g Total Fat (4.3 g Mono, 1.4 g Poly, 1.7 g Sat); 42 mg Cholesterol; 16 g Carbohydrate; 3 g Fibre; 28 g Protein; 586 mg Sodium

Make It A Meal with cooked potatoes mashed with sour cream and chopped green onion. Serve with coleslaw mix (available in your grocer's produce department) tossed with coleslaw dressing.

Paré Pointer

It's a mystery that sheep don't shrink when it rains.

Tropical Ham Dinner

*Tropical fruit salsa speckled with cilantro makes
an exotic condiment for sweet ham steak.*

PINEAPPLE MANGO SALSA

Can of pineapple tidbits, drained and juice reserved	14 oz.	398 mL
Can of sliced mango with syrup, drained, juice reserved, chopped	14 oz.	398 mL
Finely chopped red onion	1/2 cup	125 mL
Finely chopped fresh cilantro or parsley	2 tbsp.	30 mL
Lime juice	2 tbsp.	30 mL

JUICY RICE

Reserved juice from pineapple tidbits		
Reserved juice from sliced mango		
Water		
Long grain white rice	1 cup	250 mL
Chicken bouillon powder	2 tsp.	10 mL
Hard margarine (or butter)	1 tsp.	5 mL
Dijon mustard	2 tsp.	10 mL
Ham steak (about 1 lb., 454 g)	1	1
Brown sugar, packed	1 tbsp.	15 mL

Pineapple Mango Salsa: Combine all 5 ingredients in medium bowl.
Makes about 2 1/2 cups (625 mL) salsa. Set aside.

Juicy Rice: Measure 1 tbsp. (15 mL) reserved pineapple juice into small
cup. Set aside. Combine remaining pineapple juice and mango juice in
2 cup (500 mL) liquid measure. Add enough water to make 2 cups
(500 mL) liquid. Pour into medium saucepan.

Add rice, bouillon powder and margarine. Stir. Bring to a boil on high.
Reduce heat to medium-low. Cover. Simmer for 15 to 20 minutes, without
stirring, until rice is tender. Remove from heat. Fluff with fork. Cover
to keep warm. Makes about 3 cups (750 mL) rice. Meanwhile, prepare
ham steak.

(continued on next page)

Add mustard to pineapple juice in small cup. Stir until smooth. Place ham steak on greased foil-lined baking sheet. Brush with mustard mixture. Sprinkle with brown sugar. Broil 6 inches (15 cm) from heat in oven for about 5 minutes until ham is heated through and brown sugar is bubbling. Cut into 4 equal pieces. Remove to small serving plate. Add 1 1/4 cups (300 mL) Pineapple Mango Salsa to Juicy Rice. Stir well. Remove to medium serving bowl. Serve remaining salsa with ham and rice. Serves 4.

1 serving: 529 Calories; 12.3 g Total Fat (6 g Mono, 2.1 g Poly, 4 g Sat); 67 mg Cholesterol; 74 g Carbohydrate; 3 g Fibre; 31 g Protein; 2087 mg Sodium

Make It A Meal with cooked green beans dotted with margarine or butter and sprinkled with toasted sliced almonds.

Paré Pointer

These homes are all joined together, yet they're called apart-ments.

Chorizo White Bean Ragoût

This spicy dish will be just a flash in the pan once your family tastes it.
A colourful meal that's on the table in no time.

Cooking oil	1/2 tsp.	2 mL
Chorizo sausages, casings removed, chopped	1 1/2 lbs.	680 g
Chopped red onion	1 cup	250 mL
Can of diced tomatoes (with juice)	14 oz.	398 mL
Balsamic vinegar	2 tsp.	10 mL
Granulated sugar	1 tsp.	5 mL
Salt	1/4 tsp.	1 mL
Can of white kidney beans, rinsed and drained	19 oz.	540 mL
Fresh asparagus, trimmed of tough ends, cut into 1 inch (2.5 cm) pieces	1 lb.	454 g
Chopped fresh parsley	1/4 cup	60 mL

Heat cooking oil in large frying pan on medium-high. Add sausage. Scramble-fry for about 5 minutes until browned. Drain, reserving about 1 tsp. (5 mL) drippings in pan.

Add onion. Cook on medium for 5 to 10 minutes, stirring often, until onion is softened.

Meanwhile, combine next 4 ingredients in medium bowl. Add to sausage mixture. Stir. Bring to a boil. Boil, uncovered, for 5 to 10 minutes, stirring occasionally, until slightly thickened.

Add remaining 3 ingredients. Stir. Cover. Cook for 3 to 5 minutes until asparagus is tender-crisp. Serves 6.

1 serving: 265 Calories; 15 g Total Fat (6.9 g Mono, 2 g Poly, 5.2 g Sat); 42 mg Cholesterol; 17 g Carbohydrate; 5 g Fibre; 16 g Protein; 697 mg Sodium

Pictured on page 90.

Make It A Meal with sliced ready-made polenta brushed with olive oil. Brown on greased electric grill or in greased frying pan.

Dilly Pork Stir-Fry

A tasty dish with a "dilly-cious" lemon twist. Not your average stir-fry!

Water	1/4 cup	60 mL
Milk	1/4 cup	60 mL
Cornstarch	1 tbsp.	15 mL
Dill weed	2 tsp.	10 mL
Chicken bouillon powder	1 tsp.	5 mL
Lemon juice	1/2 tsp.	2 mL
Garlic powder	1/4 tsp.	1 mL
Cooking oil	1 tbsp.	15 mL
Thinly sliced carrot	1 1/4 cups	300 mL
Snow peas, trimmed	2 cups	500 mL
Sliced leek (white part only)	1 cup	250 mL
Cooking oil	1 tbsp.	15 mL
Pork tenderloin, trimmed of fat, cut into thin strips (see Tip, page 13)	1 lb.	454 g
Salt	1/4 tsp.	1 mL
Pepper	1/4 tsp.	1 mL

Combine first 7 ingredients in small bowl. Set aside.

Heat wok or large frying pan on medium-high until very hot. Add first amount of cooking oil. Add carrot. Stir-fry for about 2 minutes until tender-crisp. Transfer to medium bowl. Stir-fry snow peas and leek in same wok for 1 to 2 minutes until tender-crisp. Add to carrot.

Heat second amount of cooking oil in same wok. Add pork. Stir-fry for 3 to 4 minutes until no longer pink.

Add vegetables, salt and pepper. Stir. Stir cornstarch mixture. Add to pork mixture. Heat and stir for about 1 minute until sauce is boiling and thickened. Serves 4.

1 serving: 298 Calories; 12.4 g Total Fat (6.4 g Mono, 2.8 g Poly, 2.3 g Sat); 72 mg Cholesterol; 18 g Carbohydrate; 3 g Fibre; 28 g Protein; 421 mg Sodium

Pictured on page 72.

Make It A Meal with hot long grain rice, or pick up some ready-made fried rice from a Chinese restaurant on the way home.

Pork And Apple Skillet

Tender-crisp red cabbage and sweet apple perfectly punctuate pork.

Water	1 tbsp.	15 mL
Cornstarch	2 tsp.	10 mL
Cooking oil	1 tbsp.	15 mL
Pork tenderloin, trimmed of fat, thinly sliced (see Tip, page 13)	1 lb.	454 g
Salt, sprinkle		
Pepper, sprinkle		
Shredded red cabbage	2 cups	500 mL
Medium cooking apple (such as McIntosh), peeled, core removed, chopped	1	1
Apple juice	2/3 cup	150 mL
Lemon pepper	1/2 tsp.	2 mL
Dried thyme (or 1 tsp., 5 mL, fresh)	1/4 tsp.	1 mL
Precooked bacon slices, chopped	6	6
Toasted walnut pieces (see Tip, page 46)	1/4 cup	60 mL

Stir water into cornstarch in small cup until smooth. Set aside.

Heat cooking oil in large frying pan on medium-high. Add pork, salt and pepper. Cook for 5 to 10 minutes, stirring occasionally, until pork starts to brown.

Add next 5 ingredients. Stir. Cook, uncovered, for about 5 minutes, stirring occasionally, until cabbage is tender-crisp.

Stir cornstarch mixture. Add to pork mixture. Add bacon and walnuts. Heat and stir for about 1 minute until sauce is boiling and thickened. Serves 4.

1 serving: 337 Calories; 18.1 g Total Fat (7.6 g Mono, 5.3 g Poly, 4 g Sat); 80 mg Cholesterol; 15 g Carbohydrate; 2 g Fibre; 29 g Protein; 293 mg Sodium

Make It A Meal with cooked potatoes mashed with butter or margarine and sautéed minced garlic. Sprinkle with chopped fresh parsley.

Peach Peppercorn Pork

A delightful dish that beckons you. One taste
and you'll agree—it's just peachy!

Cooking oil	1 tsp.	5 mL
Bone-in pork chops (about 1 1/4 lbs., 560 g), trimmed of fat	4	4
Prepared chicken broth	2/3 cup	150 mL
All-purpose flour	1 tbsp.	15 mL
Can of sliced peaches in light syrup, drained and chopped	14 oz.	398 mL
Can of green peppercorns, drained	2 oz.	55 g
Medium sherry	2 tbsp.	30 mL
Apple cider vinegar	2 tsp.	10 mL
Dried thyme	1/2 tsp.	2 mL
Finely chopped onion	1/2 cup	125 mL

Heat cooking oil in large frying pan on medium. Add pork chops. Cook for 5 to 6 minutes per side until desired doneness. Transfer to large serving platter. Cover to keep warm.

Meanwhile, stir broth into flour in small bowl until smooth. Set aside.

Combine next 5 ingredients in separate small bowl. Set aside.

Cook onion in same large frying pan on medium for 5 to 10 minutes, stirring often, until softened. Add peach mixture. Heat and stir for 1 minute, scraping any brown bits from bottom of pan. Stir flour mixture. Add to peach mixture. Heat and stir for about 3 minutes until boiling and thickened. Spoon onto pork chops. Serves 4.

1 serving: 250 Calories; 7.8 g Total Fat (3.6 g Mono, 1.2 g Poly, 2.3 g Sat); 63 mg Cholesterol; 20 g Carbohydrate; 1 g Fibre; 25 g Protein; 201 mg Sodium

Make It A Meal with hot long grain rice tossed with sautéed diced red pepper and toasted slivered almonds. Serve with steamed green beans.

Paré Pointer

His mind was wandering, but it's too small to be out alone.

Hash Brown Pork Skillet

*Hash brown potatoes go for a "wok" with pork in this
mildly seasoned one-dish dinner.*

Prepared beef broth	3/4 cup	175 mL
Cornstarch	1 tbsp.	15 mL
Ketchup	2 tbsp.	30 mL
Dried whole oregano	1/2 tsp.	2 mL
Garlic powder	1/4 tsp.	1 mL
Salt	1/4 tsp.	1 mL
Pepper	1/4 tsp.	1 mL
Cooking oil	1 tbsp.	15 mL
Boneless centre-cut pork chops, cut into thin strips (see Tip, page 13)	3/4 lb.	340 g
Cooking oil	2 tsp.	10 mL
Thinly sliced onion	1/2 cup	125 mL
Frozen hash brown potatoes	3 cups	750 mL
Thinly sliced carrot	1 cup	250 mL
Thinly sliced celery	1/4 cup	60 mL
Frozen french-style green beans, thawed	1 cup	250 mL

Combine first 7 ingredients in small bowl. Set aside.

Heat wok or large frying pan on medium-high until very hot. Add first
amount of cooking oil. Add pork. Stir-fry for about 3 minutes until starting
to brown. Transfer to medium bowl.

Heat second amount of cooking oil in same wok. Add onion. Stir-fry for
1 minute.

Add hash brown potatoes, carrot and celery. Cook for about 4 minutes,
stirring often, until vegetables are tender-crisp and potatoes start to brown.

Add pork and green beans. Stir. Stir cornstarch mixture. Add to pork
mixture. Heat and stir on medium for about 2 minutes until sauce is boiling
and thickened and green beans are tender-crisp. Serves 4.

*1 serving: 399 Calories; 15.9 g Total Fat (7.4 g Mono, 3.2 g Poly, 3.8 g Sat); 57 mg Cholesterol;
42 g Carbohydrate; 5 g Fibre; 23 g Protein; 518 mg Sodium*

Make It A Meal with pickled beets and wedges of tomato sprinkled with
freshly ground pepper.

Breaded Pork Cutlets

No need to get into a snit about what to make for dinner
when you can quickly get into a schnitzel instead!

Fine dry bread crumbs	3/4 cup	175 mL
Parsley flakes	1 tbsp.	15 mL
Grated lemon zest	2 tsp.	10 mL
Salt	1 tsp.	5 mL
Pepper	1/2 tsp.	2 mL
Large egg	1	1
Water	2 tbsp.	30 mL
Pork shoulder butt cutlets (about 1 lb., 454 g), see Note	4	4
Cooking oil	1 tbsp.	15 mL
Cooking oil (optional)	1/2 tbsp.	7 mL

Lemon wedges, for garnish

Combine first 5 ingredients in small bowl. Spread evenly on sheet of waxed paper.

Beat egg and water with fork in small shallow dish.

Dip each pork cutlet in egg mixture. Press both sides of each cutlet into bread crumb mixture until coated. Heat first amount of cooking oil in large frying pan on medium. Add cutlets. Cook for 3 to 4 minutes per side, adding second amount of cooking oil if necessary to prevent sticking, until desired doneness.

Garnish individual servings with lemon wedges. Serves 4.

1 serving: 412 Calories; 26.7 g Total Fat (12.2 g Mono, 3.8 g Poly, 8.1 g Sat); 121 mg Cholesterol; 16 g Carbohydrate; 1 g Fibre; 25 g Protein; 867 mg Sodium

Note: If tenderized pork shoulder butt cutlets are unavailable, purchase 4 boneless pork loin chops. Place chops between 2 sheets of plastic wrap. Pound with meat mallet until about 1/4 inch (6 mm) thick.

Make It A Meal with frozen perogies cooked according to package directions and served with sour cream. Steam coarsely chopped cabbage until tender-crisp and toss with margarine or butter, salt and pepper.

Sesame Pork Stir-Fry

Tender pork and onion glisten with golden ginger sauce.
A sprinkling of sesame seeds makes this simply sensational.

Prepared chicken broth	1/3 cup	75 mL
Hoisin sauce	3 tbsp.	50 mL
Low-sodium soy sauce	1 1/2 tbsp.	25 mL
Cornstarch	2 tsp.	10 mL
Cooking oil	1 tbsp.	15 mL
Pork tenderloin, trimmed of fat, cut into thin strips (see Tip, page 13)	1 lb.	454 g
Cooking oil	1 tbsp.	15 mL
Medium onions, cut into thin wedges	2	2
Finely grated, peeled gingerroot	2 tsp.	10 mL
Toasted sesame seeds (see Tip, page 46)	2 tsp.	10 mL

Combine first 4 ingredients in small bowl. Set aside.

Heat wok or large frying pan on medium-high until very hot. Add first amount of cooking oil. Add pork. Stir-fry for about 5 minutes until starting to brown. Transfer to large plate.

Heat second amount of cooking oil in same wok. Add onion and ginger. Stir-fry for about 3 minutes until onion is tender-crisp. Stir cornstarch mixture. Add to onion mixture. Add pork. Heat and stir for about 1 minute until sauce is boiling and thickened.

Sprinkle with sesame seeds. Serves 4.

1 serving: 277 Calories; 10.8 g Total Fat (5.7 g Mono, 2.8 g Poly, 1.7 g Sat); 67 mg Cholesterol; 15 g Carbohydrate; 1 g Fibre; 29 g Protein; 612 mg Sodium

Make It A Meal with chow mein noodles cooked according to package directions, tossed with a small amount of sesame oil and chopped green onion. Serve with a mixture of steamed sugar snap peas and sliced carrots.

Greek Lamb And Feta

*When you're in the mood for something just
a little different, this fits the bill.*

Crumbled feta cheese (about 2 1/2 oz., 70 g)	1/2 cup	125 mL
Chopped tomato	1/4 cup	60 mL
Chopped walnuts	1/4 cup	60 mL
Cooking oil	1 tsp.	5 mL
Lean ground lamb	1 lb.	454 g
Chopped onion	1/2 cup	125 mL
Can of tomato paste	5 1/2 oz.	156 mL
Dry red (or alcohol-free) wine	1/4 cup	60 mL
Water	1/4 cup	60 mL
Lemon juice	2 tbsp.	30 mL
Granulated sugar	1 tsp.	5 mL
Dried whole oregano	1/2 tsp.	2 mL
Ground cinnamon	1/4 tsp.	1 mL
Ground cumin	1/4 tsp.	1 mL
Box of frozen chopped spinach, thawed and squeezed dry	10 oz.	300 g
Grated lemon zest	1/2 tsp.	2 mL

Combine cheese, tomato and walnuts in small bowl. Set aside.

Heat cooking oil in large frying pan on medium-high. Add ground lamb and onion. Scramble-fry for 5 to 10 minutes until lamb is no longer pink and onion is softened. Drain.

Add next 8 ingredients. Stir well. Bring to a boil. Reduce heat to medium. Simmer, uncovered, for 5 minutes, stirring occasionally, to blend flavours.

Add spinach and lemon zest. Stir. Cover. Cook for about 3 minutes, stirring occasionally, until heated through. Remove to large serving bowl. Sprinkle with cheese mixture. Serves 4.

1 serving: 411 Calories; 26.2 g Total Fat (9.3 g Mono, 4.9 g Poly, 9.9 g Sat); 94 mg Cholesterol; 16 g Carbohydrate; 4 g Fibre; 28 g Protein; 353 mg Sodium

Make It A Meal with pita bread wedges, cucumber slices and your favourite olives.

Peppered Lamb Chops

Vegetables colourfully complement seasoned lamb chops
in this easy-to-make entrée.

Olive (or cooking) oil	2 tbsp.	30 mL
Balsamic vinegar	2 tbsp.	30 mL
Salt	1/4 tsp.	1 mL
Lamb loin chops (about 2 lbs., 900 g)	8	8
Coarse ground pepper	1 1/2 tsp.	7 mL
Olive (or cooking) oil	1 tbsp.	15 mL
Sliced red pepper	1 1/2 cups	375 mL
Thinly sliced onion	1 cup	250 mL
Brown sugar, packed	1 tsp.	5 mL
Salt	1/4 tsp.	1 mL
Fresh spinach leaves, lightly packed	3 cups	750 mL

Beat first 3 ingredients with fork in small cup.

Heat large frying pan on medium until hot. Brush both sides of each lamb chop with olive oil mixture. Reserve any remaining olive oil mixture. Sprinkle both sides of each chop with pepper. Add to pan. Cook for about 6 minutes per side, brushing with reserved olive oil mixture, until desired doneness. Transfer to large plate. Cover to keep warm.

Heat second amount of olive oil in same large frying pan. Add red pepper and onion. Cover. Cook for about 3 minutes, stirring occasionally, until tender-crisp.

Add brown sugar and second amount of salt. Heat and stir for about 1 minute until brown sugar is dissolved.

Add spinach. Heat and stir for about 1 minute until spinach is wilted. Remove to large serving platter. Arrange lamb chops on top. Serves 4.

1 serving: 314 Calories; 17.9 g Total Fat (10.5 g Mono, 1.7 g Poly, 4 g Sat); 80 mg Cholesterol; 11 g Carbohydrate; 3 g Fibre; 28 g Protein; 418 mg Sodium

Pictured on page 71.

Make It A Meal with cooked yam mashed with sour cream, nutmeg, salt and pepper.

Rosemary Peppered Lamb

Rich rosemary-infused "jus" coats tender lamb chops
in this simply delicious combination.

All-purpose flour	2 tbsp.	30 mL
Rack of lamb with 8 ribs, cut between ribs into 8 chops	1 1/2 lbs.	680 g
Cooking oil	1 tbsp.	15 mL
Thinly sliced onion	1 cup	250 mL
Thinly sliced carrot	1 cup	250 mL
Dry red (or alcohol-free) wine	1/2 cup	125 mL
Prepared chicken (or beef) broth	1/2 cup	125 mL
Sprigs of fresh rosemary	2	2
Coarse ground pepper	1 tsp.	5 mL
Salt	1/4 tsp.	1 mL

Measure flour into large resealable freezer bag. Add 2 lamb chops. Seal bag. Toss until coated. Repeat with remaining chops.

Heat cooking oil in large frying pan on medium-high. Add chops. Cook for about 2 minutes per side until browned. Transfer to large plate. Cover to keep warm.

Cook onion and carrot in same large frying pan on medium for 5 to 10 minutes, stirring often, until onion is softened.

Add remaining 5 ingredients. Stir. Bring to a boil. Boil gently, uncovered, for 2 minutes, stirring occasionally, to blend flavours. Add chops. Turn until coated with sauce. Cook, uncovered, for about 3 minutes until desired doneness. Discard rosemary sprigs. Serves 4.

1 serving: 526 Calories; 39.7 g Total Fat (16.9 g Mono, 3.9 g Poly, 16.2 g Sat); 100 mg Cholesterol; 12 g Carbohydrate; 2 g Fibre; 24 g Protein; 356 mg Sodium

Make It A Meal with sliced ready-made polenta cooked according to package directions. Sprinkle with melted margarine or butter, grated Parmesan cheese, chopped fresh parsley and pepper for extra flavour. Serve with cooked Brussels sprouts tossed with margarine or butter, liquid honey and a squeeze of lemon.

Thai-Style Lamb Chops

A fabulous fusion of flavours that tastes like you've been cooking for hours.

Sweet chili sauce	1/3 cup	75 mL
Chopped fresh cilantro or parsley	2 tbsp.	30 mL
Lime juice	1 tbsp.	15 mL
Fish sauce	2 tsp.	10 mL
Grated lime zest	1 tsp.	5 mL
Garlic cloves, minced (or 1/2 tsp., 2 mL, powder)	2	2
Rack of lamb with 8 ribs, cut between ribs into 8 chops	1 1/2 lbs.	680 g

Preheat broiler. Combine first 6 ingredients in small bowl.

Spread chili sauce mixture on both sides of each lamb chop. Place chops on greased wire rack set in foil-lined baking sheet with sides. Broil 6 inches (15 cm) from heat in oven for 4 to 5 minutes per side until desired doneness. Serves 4.

1 serving: 376 Calories; 29.6 g Total Fat (12.1 g Mono, 2.3 g Poly, 13.1 g Sat); 82 mg Cholesterol; 7 g Carbohydrate; 2 g Fibre; 19 g Protein; 645 mg Sodium

Pictured on page 71.

Make It A Meal with hot wild rice mix. Microwave frozen Oriental mixed vegetables according to package directions and toss with a small amount of soy sauce and sesame oil.

1. Peppered Lamb Chops, page 68
2. Thai-Style Lamb Chops, above

Props courtesy of: Cherison Enterprises Inc.

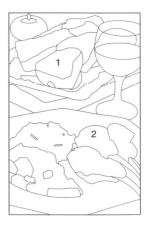

Chili Pork

Ground pork and taco seasoning make this chili just a bit different.
Serve with tortilla chips, salsa and sour cream.

Cooking oil	1 tsp.	5 mL
Lean ground pork	1 lb.	454 g
Chopped onion	1 cup	250 mL
Chopped green pepper	1 cup	250 mL
Can of red kidney beans, rinsed and drained	19 oz.	540 mL
Can of diced tomatoes (with juice)	14 oz.	398 mL
Dry white (or alcohol-free) wine	1/2 cup	125 mL
Taco seasoning mix, stir before measuring	3 tbsp.	50 mL
Tomato paste (see Tip, page 75)	2 tbsp.	30 mL

Heat cooking oil in large saucepan on medium-high. Add ground pork, onion and green pepper. Scramble-fry for 5 to 10 minutes until pork is no longer pink and vegetables are softened. Drain.

Add remaining 5 ingredients. Stir. Reduce heat to medium. Cook, uncovered, for about 10 minutes, stirring occasionally, until thickened. Serves 6.

1 serving: 285 Calories; 12.5 g Total Fat (5.3 g Mono, 1.5 g Poly, 4.2 g Sat); 49 mg Cholesterol; 22 g Carbohydrate; 5 g Fibre; 19 g Protein; 1049 mg Sodium

Make It A Meal with a salad of sliced English cucumber (with peel) and chopped fresh mint tossed with a vinaigrette made of equal parts cooking oil and white wine vinegar.

1. Dilly Pork Stir-Fry, page 61
2. Orange Ginger Pork Chops, page 76

Props courtesy of: Casa Bugatti

Pork Stroganoff

Red wine adds a subtle accent to saucy pork. Goes well with rice or noodles.

Cooking oil	2 tsp.	10 mL
Pork tenderloin, trimmed of fat, cut across grain into thin strips (see Tip, page 13)	1 lb.	454 g
Cooking oil	1 tbsp.	15 mL
Sliced fresh white mushrooms	3 cups	750 mL
Thinly sliced onion	1 1/2 cups	375 mL
Garlic cloves, minced (or 1/2 tsp., 2 mL, powder)	2	2
Prepared beef broth	1 cup	250 mL
Dry red (or alcohol-free) wine	1/3 cup	75 mL
Tomato paste (see Tip, page 75)	1/4 cup	60 mL
Paprika	2 tsp.	10 mL
Sour cream	1/3 cup	75 mL
Parsley flakes (or 2 tbsp., 30 mL, chopped fresh parsley)	1 1/2 tsp.	7 mL

Heat first amount of cooking oil in large frying pan on medium-high. Add pork. Cook for about 5 minutes, stirring often, until browned. Transfer to large plate.

Heat second amount of cooking oil in same large frying pan on medium. Add mushrooms, onion and garlic. Cook for 5 to 10 minutes, stirring often, until onion is softened and liquid is evaporated.

Add pork and next 4 ingredients. Stir. Bring to a boil. Reduce heat to medium-low. Simmer, uncovered, for 5 to 10 minutes, stirring occasionally, until pork is tender and sauce is slightly thickened.

Add sour cream and parsley. Stir well. Serves 4.

(continued on next page)

1 serving: 305 Calories; 14.2 g Total Fat (6.5 g Mono, 2.6 g Poly, 4 g Sat); 79 mg Cholesterol; 14 g Carbohydrate; 3 g Fibre; 28 g Protein; 291 mg Sodium

Make It A Meal with hot buttered egg noodles. Add a side dish of shredded red cabbage cooked in a mixture of 1 to 2 tbsp. (15 to 30 mL) each brown sugar, white vinegar, water and hard margarine or butter until tender-crisp.

 If a recipe calls for less than an entire can of tomato paste, freeze unopened can for 30 minutes. Open both ends and push contents through one end. Slice off only what you need. Freeze remaining paste in resealable freezer bag or plastic wrap for future use.

Orange Ginger Pork Chops

A tasty bit of the Orient! Thick, tangy sauce is nice with rice.

Orange juice	1/2 cup	125 mL
Prepared chicken broth	1/2 cup	125 mL
Cornstarch	1 tbsp.	15 mL
Brown sugar, packed	2 tsp.	10 mL
Garlic clove, minced (or 1/4 tsp., 1 mL, powder)	1	1
Cooking oil	2 tsp.	10 mL
Boneless pork loin chops (about 1 lb., 454 g), trimmed of fat	4	4
Can of mandarin orange segments, drained and juice reserved (see Note)	10 oz.	284 mL
Chopped pickled ginger slices, drained	2 tbsp.	30 mL
Sliced green onion	2 tbsp.	30 mL

Combine first 5 ingredients in medium bowl. Set aside.

Heat cooking oil in large frying pan on medium-high. Add pork chops. Cook for about 2 minutes per side until browned. Transfer chops to plate. Reduce heat to medium-low. Stir cornstarch mixture. Add to frying pan. Stir gently.

Add orange segments and ginger. Stir gently. Add chops. Cook, uncovered, for about 5 minutes, turning chops at halftime, until desired doneness and sauce is boiling and thickened. Remove to large serving dish.

Sprinkle with green onion. Serves 4.

1 serving: 242 Calories; 9.1 g Total Fat (4.4 g Mono, 1.5 g Poly, 2.5 g Sat); 67 mg Cholesterol; 13 g Carbohydrate; 1 g Fibre; 26 g Protein; 164 mg Sodium

Pictured on page 72.

Note: Use mandarin orange juice to cook rice or use in your favourite dessert recipe.

Make It A Meal with a salad of grated cabbage and carrot tossed with an oriental ginger dressing. Serve with rice cooked in juice from the mandarin orange segments and low-sodium chicken broth.

Pork & Lamb

Honey Pork And Cabbage

Asian-inspired and subtly sweetened with honey.
Great with noodles or rice.

Prepared chicken broth	1/4 cup	60 mL
Hoisin sauce	2 tbsp.	30 mL
Liquid honey	2 tbsp.	30 mL
Cornstarch	1 tbsp.	15 mL
Chili paste (sambal oelek)	1 tsp.	5 mL
Pepper	1/4 tsp.	1 mL
All-purpose flour	1 tbsp.	15 mL
Cornstarch	1 tbsp.	15 mL
Chinese five-spice powder	1/2 tsp.	2 mL
Boneless pork loin chops, trimmed of fat, cut into 1/4 inch (6 mm) strips (see Tip, page 13)	1 lb.	454 g
Cooking oil	2 tbsp.	30 mL
Coarsely chopped suey choy (Chinese cabbage)	8 cups	2 L

Combine first 6 ingredients in small bowl. Set aside.

Combine next 3 ingredients in medium bowl. Add pork. Stir until coated.

Heat wok or large frying pan on medium-high until very hot. Add cooking oil. Add pork mixture. Stir-fry for about 5 minutes until pork is browned and crisp. Transfer with slotted spoon to separate medium bowl. Cover to keep warm.

Add suey choy to same wok. Stir-fry for about 5 minutes until tender-crisp. Stir cornstarch mixture. Add to suey choy. Heat and stir for about 1 minute until sauce is boiling and thickened. Remove to large serving platter. Spoon pork onto suey choy. Serves 4.

1 serving: 341Calories; 15 g Total Fat (7.6 g Mono, 3.1 g Poly, 3.2 g Sat); 62 mg Cholesterol; 25 g Carbohydrate; 2 g Fibre; 28 g Protein; 320 mg Sodium

Make It A Meal with fresh Shanghai noodles cooked according to package directions. Add snow peas to noodles during the last 2 minutes of cooking time. Drain. Garnish with chopped green onion.

Stir-Fry Stew

East meets West—in the wok or in the frying pan. You decide.
Have the pork and vegetables prepared before beginning this stir-fry.

Pineapple juice	1/2 cup	125 mL
Soy sauce	3 tbsp.	50 mL
Cornstarch	2 tbsp.	30 mL
Granulated sugar	1 tsp.	5 mL
Garlic powder	1/2 tsp.	2 mL
Salt	1/2 tsp.	2 mL
Cooking oil	1 tbsp.	15 mL
Pork tenderloin, trimmed of fat, cut diagonally across grain into 1/4 inch (6 mm) slices (see Tip, page 13)	1 lb.	454 g
Chopped onion	2 cups	500 mL
Fresh vegetable stir-fry mix	5 cups	1.25 L
Medium potatoes, quartered lengthwise and sliced paper-thin	2	2
Prepared chicken broth	1 cup	250 mL

Combine first 6 ingredients in small bowl. Set aside.

Heat wok or large frying pan on medium-high until very hot. Add cooking oil. Add pork and onion. Stir-fry for about 5 minutes until pork starts to brown.

Add stir-fry mix, potato and broth. Stir. Bring to a boil. Reduce heat to medium. Cover. Simmer for about 10 minutes until vegetables are tender. Stir cornstarch mixture. Add to pork mixture. Heat and stir for about 2 minutes until sauce is boiling and thickened. Serves 4.

1 serving: 351 Calories; 9.1 g Total Fat (4.4 g Mono, 1.8 g Poly, 2.1 g Sat); 72 mg Cholesterol; 37 g Carbohydrate; 5 g Fibre; 31 g Protein; 1424 mg Sodium

Make It A Meal with heat-and-serve spring rolls or egg rolls (available in your grocer's freezer) cooked according to package directions and served with tangy sweet-and-sour or plum sauce for dipping.

Pork Marsala

Sweet marsala wine sauce complements tender pork cutlets.

Milk	1 cup	250 mL
All-purpose flour	2 tbsp.	30 mL
Marsala wine	1/3 cup	75 mL
Salt	1/4 tsp.	1 mL
Pepper	1/4 tsp.	1 mL
All-purpose flour	2 tbsp.	30 mL
Pork shoulder butt cutlets (about 1 lb., 454 g), see Note	4	4
Cooking oil	1 tbsp.	15 mL
Hard margarine (or butter)	1 tbsp.	15 mL
Dried chives (or 2 1/2 tbsp., 37 mL, chopped fresh)	2 tsp.	10 mL

Stir milk into first amount of flour in small bowl until smooth. Add wine, salt and pepper. Stir well. Set aside.

Measure second amount of flour into large resealable freezer bag. Add 2 pork cutlets. Seal bag. Toss until coated. Repeat with remaining cutlets.

Heat cooking oil and margarine in large frying pan on medium-high. Add cutlets. Cook for about 2 minutes per side until browned. Transfer to large plate. Cover to keep warm. Reduce heat to medium. Stir flour mixture. Slowly add to hot pan, stirring constantly and scraping any brown bits from bottom of pan. Heat and stir for about 3 minutes until boiling and thickened.

Add chives. Stir. Add cutlets. Turn until coated with sauce. Cover. Simmer for about 2 minutes until desired doneness. Serves 4.

1 serving: 414 Calories; 28 g Total Fat (13.4 g Mono, 3.6 g Poly, 8.5 g Sat); 70 mg Cholesterol; 12 g Carbohydrate; trace Fibre; 24 g Protein; 290 mg Sodium

Note: If tenderized pork shoulder butt cutlets are unavailable, purchase 4 boneless pork loin chops. Place chops between 2 sheets of plastic wrap. Pound with meat mallet until about 1/4 inch (6 mm) thick.

Make It A Meal with orzo (rice-shaped pasta) cooked according to package directions and tossed with sautéed chopped mushrooms, zucchini (with peel), onion and garlic. Season with Italian herbs.

Pork Steak Diane

Rich, creamy brandy sauce smothers tender pork chops.
Perfect for last-minute company.

Can of evaporated milk	13 1/2 oz.	385 mL
All-purpose flour	1 tbsp.	15 mL
Pepper, sprinkle		
Boneless pork loin chops (about 1 lb., 454 g), trimmed of fat	4	4
Cooking oil	1 tbsp.	15 mL
Hard margarine (or butter)	1 tbsp.	15 mL
Finely chopped onion	2 tbsp.	30 mL
Garlic clove, minced (or 1/4 tsp., 1 mL, powder)	1	1
Worcestershire sauce	1 tbsp.	15 mL
Brandy (see Note)	1 tbsp.	15 mL
Parsley flakes (or 1 tbsp., 15 mL, chopped fresh parsley)	3/4 tsp.	4 mL

Stir evaporated milk into flour in small bowl until smooth. Set aside.

Sprinkle pepper on both sides of each pork chop. Heat cooking oil in large frying pan on medium. Add chops. Cook for 3 to 5 minutes per side until desired doneness. Transfer to large plate. Cover to keep warm.

Melt margarine in same large frying pan. Add onion and garlic. Heat and stir for about 1 minute until fragrant.

Add Worcestershire sauce and brandy. Heat and stir for about 1 minute, scraping any brown bits from bottom of pan, until liquid is evaporated. Stir flour mixture. Add to onion mixture. Heat and stir for about 3 minutes until sauce is boiling and slightly thickened. Add chops. Turn until coated with sauce. Cook for about 1 minute until heated through. Remove chops to large serving platter. Drizzle with sauce from pan.

Sprinkle with parsley. Serves 4.

(continued on next page)

1 serving: 377 Calories; 20.4 g Total Fat (9.1 g Mono, 2.2 g Poly, 7.8 g Sat); 93 mg Cholesterol; 13 g Carbohydrate; trace Fibre; 32 g Protein; 240 mg Sodium

Note: If preferred, omit brandy. Use 1/4 tsp. (1 mL) brandy flavouring.

Make It A Meal with a Caesar salad kit (found in your grocer's produce department) and baby potatoes cooked in the microwave, cut up and tossed with sour cream and sliced green onions.

Paré Pointer

One gets so tired of doing nothing—there's never time to stop and rest.

Chili Coconut Pork

Thai-inspired flavours add pizzazz to pork!

Water	1 tbsp.	15 mL
Cornstarch	2 tsp.	10 mL
Cooking oil	1 tsp.	5 mL
Pork tenderloin, trimmed of fat, cut across grain into thin strips (see Tip, page 13)	1 lb.	454 g
Cooking oil	1 tsp.	5 mL
Sliced yellow (or red) pepper	1 1/2 cups	375 mL
Finely grated, peeled gingerroot (or 1/4 tsp., 1 mL, ground ginger)	1 tsp.	5 mL
Ground cumin	1 tsp.	5 mL
Dried crushed chilies	1/2 tsp.	2 mL
Can of light coconut milk	14 oz.	398 mL
Mango chutney	1/3 cup	75 mL
Salt	1/4 tsp.	1 mL
Frozen peas	1/2 cup	125 mL

Stir water into cornstarch in small cup until smooth. Set aside.

Heat wok or large frying pan on medium-high until very hot. Add first amount of cooking oil. Add pork. Stir-fry for 4 to 5 minutes until no longer pink. Transfer to small bowl. Cover to keep warm.

Heat second amount of cooking oil in same wok on medium. Add next 4 ingredients. Stir-fry for about 1 minute until fragrant.

Add coconut milk, chutney and salt. Stir. Bring to a boil on medium-high. Boil gently, uncovered, for 5 minutes, stirring occasionally, to blend flavours.

Add pork and peas. Stir. Stir cornstarch mixture. Add to pork mixture. Heat and stir for about 1 minute until sauce is boiling and slightly thickened. Serves 4.

1 serving: 415 Calories; 27.8 g Total Fat (4.4 g Mono, 1.5 g Poly, 19.8 g Sat); 72 mg Cholesterol; 17 g Carbohydrate; 2 g Fibre; 28 g Protein; 246 mg Sodium

Make It A Meal with hot long grain rice and a salad made of broccoli coleslaw mix and diced apple tossed with a creamy cucumber dressing.

Pork & Lamb

Garden Vegetable Frittata

A generous layer of golden cheese tops colourful, tender-crisp veggies.

Cooking oil	1 tbsp.	15 mL
Chopped zucchini (with peel)	1 cup	250 mL
Sliced fresh white mushrooms	1 cup	250 mL
Thinly sliced red pepper	1 cup	250 mL
Sliced green onion	1/2 cup	125 mL
Large eggs	8	8
Sun-dried tomato pesto	3 tbsp.	50 mL
Pepper	1/8 tsp.	0.5 mL
Grated Asiago (or your favourite) cheese	1 cup	250 mL

Heat cooking oil in large frying pan on medium-high. Add next
4 ingredients. Stir. Reduce heat to medium. Cook for about 8 minutes,
stirring occasionally, until vegetables are tender-crisp and liquid
is evaporated.

Preheat broiler. Beat eggs, pesto and pepper with whisk in medium bowl
until well combined. Pour over vegetables. Stir for 5 seconds. Spread egg
mixture evenly in pan. Reduce heat to medium-low. Cover. Cook for about
5 minutes until bottom is golden and top is almost set. Remove from heat.

Sprinkle with cheese. Broil 6 inches (15 cm) from heat in oven (see Note)
for about 4 minutes until frittata is set and cheese is golden. Cuts into
4 wedges.

*1 wedge: 310 Calories; 21.8 g Total Fat (8.4 g Mono, 2.8 g Poly, 8.1 g Sat); 158 mg Cholesterol;
9 g Carbohydrate; 2 g Fibre; 21 g Protein; 268 mg Sodium*

Pictured on page 89.

Note: To avoid damaging frying pan handle in oven, wrap handle with foil
before placing under broiler.

Make It A Meal with steamed broccoli and cauliflower florets tossed with
pecan pieces sautéed in margarine or butter.

Chop-Chop Teriyaki Tofu

When dinner needs to be on the table quickly,
pull out your wok or frying pan and make this tasty tofu stir-fry.

Teriyaki sauce	1/2 cup	125 mL
Brown sugar, packed	1 tsp.	5 mL
Package of firm tofu, diced	12 1/4 oz.	350 g
Water	1 tbsp.	15 mL
Cornstarch	2 tsp.	10 mL
Cooking oil	2 tsp.	10 mL
Chopped onion	1/2 cup	125 mL
Garlic clove, minced (or 1/4 tsp., 1 mL, powder)	1	1
Finely grated, peeled gingerroot (or 1/4 tsp., 1 mL, ground ginger)	1 tsp.	5 mL
Frozen California vegetable mix, thawed	2 cups	500 mL
Chopped fresh cilantro or parsley (optional)	1 tbsp.	15 mL

Combine teriyaki sauce and brown sugar in medium bowl. Add tofu. Stir gently until coated. Cover. Marinate in refrigerator for 10 minutes.

Meanwhile, stir water into cornstarch in small cup until smooth. Set aside.

Heat cooking oil in wok or large frying pan on medium-high until very hot. Add onion, garlic and ginger. Stir-fry for 2 to 3 minutes until onion starts to soften.

Add vegetable mix. Stir-fry for 2 to 3 minutes until onion is softened. Add tofu with marinade. Stir gently. Stir cornstarch mixture. Add to tofu mixture. Heat and stir on low for 3 to 4 minutes until tofu is heated through and sauce is boiling and thickened. Remove to large serving bowl.

Sprinkle with cilantro. Serves 4.

1 serving: 222 Calories; 10.1 g Total Fat (3.1 g Mono, 5.1 g Poly, 1.3 g Sat); 0 mg Cholesterol; 20 g Carbohydrate; 3 g Fibre; 17 g Protein; 1493 mg Sodium

Make It A Meal with fresh Chinese egg noodles cooked according to package directions, then fried with chopped brown mushrooms and a small amount of sesame oil.

Peanut Ginger Pasta

*Chunky vegetables and crunchy peanuts make
this peppery pasta positively perfect!*

Spaghetti	10 oz.	285 g
Boiling water	8 cups	2 L
Salt	1 tsp.	5 mL
Low-sodium prepared chicken broth (or water)	1/2 cup	125 mL
Smooth peanut butter	6 tbsp.	100 mL
Soy sauce	2 tbsp.	30 mL
Liquid honey	2 tbsp.	30 mL
Dried crushed chilies	1/2 tsp.	2 mL
Cooking oil	1 tbsp.	15 mL
Fresh vegetable stir-fry mix	3 cups	750 mL
Finely grated, peeled gingerroot (or 1/2 tsp., 2 mL, ground ginger)	2 tsp.	10 mL
Chopped unsalted peanuts (optional)	3 tbsp.	50 mL

Cook spaghetti in boiling water and salt in large uncovered pot or Dutch oven for 8 to 10 minutes, stirring occasionally, until tender but firm. Drain. Return to same pot. Cover to keep warm.

Meanwhile, combine next 5 ingredients in small bowl. Set aside.

Heat wok or large frying pan on medium-high until very hot. Add cooking oil. Add stir-fry mix and ginger. Stir-fry for 3 to 4 minutes until vegetables are tender-crisp. Add broth mixture. Heat and stir until vegetables are coated. Cover. Cook for 2 to 3 minutes until vegetables are tender. Add spaghetti. Toss well. Remove to large serving dish.

Sprinkle with peanuts. Serves 4.

1 serving: 495 Calories; 17.3 g Total Fat (8.1 g Mono, 5 g Poly, 3 g Sat); 0 mg Cholesterol; 71 g Carbohydrate; 5 g Fibre; 18 g Protein; 761 mg Sodium

Make It A Meal with veggie sausages or patties (available in your grocer's freezer) cooked according to package directions.

Paré Pointer
Swimming pool sign reads: "If you drink, don't dive."

Red And Green Pasta

A colourful dish to present on a platter. Looks great at Christmas,
tastes great any time of the year.

Spaghetti	1/2 lb.	225 g
Boiling water	8 cups	2 L
Salt	1 tsp.	5 mL
Cooking oil	1/2 tsp.	2 mL
Sliced red onion	1 cup	250 mL
Garlic cloves, minced (or 1/2 tsp., 2 mL, powder)	2	2
Grape (or cherry) tomatoes	1/2 lb.	225 g
Dry white (or alcohol-free) wine	1/3 cup	75 mL
Olive oil	1/4 cup	60 mL
Dijon mustard (with whole seeds)	1 tbsp.	15 mL
Dried crushed chilies	1/2 tsp.	2 mL
Pepper	1/2 tsp.	2 mL
Bag of baby spinach	6 oz.	170 g
Chopped fresh basil	2 tbsp.	30 mL
Salt	1/4 tsp.	1 mL
Grated Parmesan cheese (optional)	1/3 cup	75 mL

Cook spaghetti in boiling water and first amount of salt in large uncovered pot or Dutch oven for 8 to 10 minutes, stirring occasionally, until tender but firm. Drain. Return to same pot. Cover to keep warm.

Meanwhile, heat cooking oil in large frying pan on medium-high. Add onion and garlic. Cook for 5 to 10 minutes, stirring often, until onion is softened.

Add tomatoes. Heat and stir for about 2 minutes until tomatoes start to soften.

Add next 5 ingredients. Heat and stir for about 2 minutes until heated through.

Add spinach, basil and second amount of salt. Heat and stir on medium for about 1 minute until spinach is wilted. Add to spaghetti. Toss well. Remove to large serving platter.

(continued on next page)

86 Meatless

Sprinkle with Parmesan cheese. Serves 4.

1 serving: 400 Calories; 16.6 g Total Fat (11.1 g Mono, 2.1 g Poly, 2.2 g Sat); 0 mg Cholesterol; 51 g Carbohydrate; 4 g Fibre; 10 g Protein; 249 mg Sodium

Make It A Meal with ciabatta bread slices and a Caesar salad kit (available in your grocer's produce department).

Southwestern Skillet Dip

*A fun and tasty one-dish meal the whole family will love.
Serve with tortilla chips and dip in!*

Chopped onion	2 cups	500 mL
Can of diced tomatoes (with juice)	14 oz.	398 mL
Chopped green pepper	1 1/2 cups	375 mL
Taco seasoning mix, stir before measuring	2 tbsp.	30 mL
Balsamic vinegar	1 tbsp.	15 mL
Granulated sugar	1 tsp.	5 mL
Can of red kidney beans, rinsed and drained	14 oz.	398 mL
Frozen kernel corn, thawed	1/2 cup	125 mL
Sour cream	1/2 cup	125 mL
Grated medium Cheddar cheese	1/2 cup	125 mL

Heat large frying pan on medium-high until hot. Add first 6 ingredients. Stir. Cook, uncovered, for 5 to 10 minutes, stirring often, until onion is softened and mixture is thickened.

Preheat broiler. Add kidney beans and corn to tomato mixture. Heat and stir for about 3 minutes until heated through. Remove from heat.

Spoon sour cream, using 1 tbsp. (15 mL) mounds, onto bean mixture. Do not stir. Sprinkle with cheese. Broil 6 inches (15 cm) from heat in oven (see Note) for about 4 minutes until cheese is melted and golden. Serves 4.

1 serving: 282 Calories; 10.3 g Total Fat (2.8 g Mono, 0.8 g Poly, 5.9 g Sat); 28 mg Cholesterol; 38 g Carbohydrate; 7 g Fibre; 13 g Protein; 1308 mg Sodium

Note: To avoid damaging frying pan handle in oven, wrap handle with foil before placing under broiler.

Make It A Meal with tortilla chips for dipping, and mixed green salad tossed with a buttermilk dressing.

Peppy Personal Pizzas

This thin-crust pizza with colourful veggie toppings
smothered in tangy cheese makes a delightful dinner.

Flour tortillas (9 inch, 22 cm, diameter)	4	4
Can of pizza sauce	7 1/2 oz.	213 mL
Sliced fresh white mushrooms	3/4 cup	175 mL
Thinly sliced red pepper	3/4 cup	175 mL
Thinly sliced green pepper	3/4 cup	175 mL
Thinly sliced red onion	1/2 cup	125 mL
Crumbled feta cheese (about 5 oz., 140 g)	1 cup	250 mL
Grated havarti cheese	1 cup	250 mL

Preheat oven to 425°F (220°C). Place tortillas on 2 greased baking sheets. Spread pizza sauce evenly on each tortilla.

Divide and layer remaining 6 ingredients, in order given, on top of sauce. Bake on separate racks in oven for about 15 minutes, switching position of baking sheets at halftime, until cheese is melted and edges are golden. Makes 4 pizzas.

1 pizza: 423 Calories; 22.1 g Total Fat (6.5 g Mono, 2.4 g Poly, 12 g Sat); 67 mg Cholesterol; 39 g Carbohydrate; 3 g Fibre; 19g Protein; 1146 mg Sodium

Pictured on page 36.

Make It A Meal with a salad of mixed greens, chopped tomato and cucumber drizzled with a ranch-style dressing.

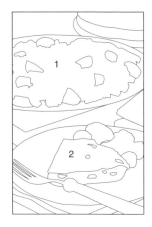

1. Pasta Primavera, page 92
2. Garden Vegetable Frittata, page 83

Props courtesy of: Island Pottery Inc.

Antipasto Pizza

Enjoy the flavours of the Mediterranean with this two-cheese-and-veggie pizza.

Prebaked pizza crust (12 inch, 30 cm, diameter)	1	1
Pizza sauce	1/2 cup	125 mL
Dried basil	1 1/2 tsp.	7 mL
Roasted red peppers, drained, blotted dry, cut into strips	1 cup	250 mL
Jar of marinated artichokes, drained and chopped	6 oz.	170 mL
Thinly sliced red onion	1/3 cup	75 mL
Chopped olives (your choice)	3 tbsp.	50 mL
Grated Parmesan cheese	1/3 cup	75 mL
Goat (chèvre) cheese, cut up	2 oz.	57 g

Preheat oven to 475°F (240°C). Place pizza crust on greased 12 inch (30 cm) pizza pan. Spread pizza sauce evenly on crust. Sprinkle with basil.

Scatter next 4 ingredients, in order given, over top.

Sprinkle with both cheeses. Bake for about 15 minutes until cheese is melted and crust is crisp and golden. Cuts into 8 wedges.

1 wedge: 169 Calories; 5.6 g Total Fat (1.4 g Mono, 0.4 g Poly, 2.5 g Sat); 9 mg Cholesterol; 22 g Carbohydrate; 2 g Fibre; 8 g Protein; 435 mg Sodium

Pictured on front cover.

Make It A Meal with a salad of fresh spinach leaves, sliced mushrooms and grated Cheddar cheese tossed with a tangy buttermilk or yogurt dressing.

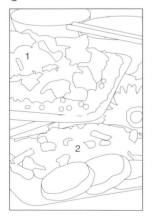

1. Broccoli Shrimp Stir-Fry, page 47
2. Chorizo White Bean Ragoût, page 60

Props courtesy of: Danesco Inc.-

Pasta Primavera

Colourful and creamy, this pasta dish will surely satisfy.

Rotini (or other spiral) pasta (about 8 oz., 225 g)	3 cups	750 mL
Boiling water	10 cups	2.5 L
Salt	1 1/4 tsp.	6 mL
Homogenized milk	1 1/2 cups	375 mL
All-purpose flour	2 tbsp.	30 mL
Cooking oil	2 tsp.	10 mL
Garlic cloves, minced (or 1/2 tsp., 2 mL, powder)	2	2
Frozen California vegetable mix, thawed and larger pieces halved	2 cups	500 mL
Sliced green onion	1/4 cup	60 mL
Pepper	1/2 tsp.	2 mL
Grated Parmesan cheese	2 tbsp.	30 mL
Cherry tomatoes, halved	6 oz.	170 g
Chopped fresh basil	1 tbsp.	15 mL
Grated Parmesan cheese	1 tbsp.	15 mL

Cook pasta in boiling water and salt in large uncovered pot or Dutch oven for 10 to 12 minutes, stirring occasionally, until tender but firm. Drain. Return to same pot. Cover to keep warm.

Meanwhile, stir milk into flour in small bowl until smooth. Set aside.

Heat cooking oil in large frying pan on medium. Add garlic. Heat and stir for about 1 minute until fragrant.

Add next 3 ingredients. Stir. Cover. Cook for 2 to 3 minutes, stirring once, until vegetables are heated through. Stir flour mixture. Add to vegetables. Heat and stir for about 2 minutes until sauce is boiling and thickened. Reduce heat to medium-low. Cover. Simmer for 5 minutes, stirring occasionally.

(continued on next page)

Add first amount of Parmesan cheese. Stir. Remove from heat. Add to pasta.

Add tomato and basil. Toss gently. Remove to large serving dish.

Sprinkle with second amount of Parmesan cheese. Serves 4.

1 serving: 370 Calories; 8.3 g Total Fat (2.9 g Mono, 1.4 g Poly, 3.3 g Sat); 17 mg Cholesterol; 60 g Carbohydrate; 4 g Fibre; 15 g Protein; 169 mg Sodium

Pictured on page 89.

Make It A Meal with heat-and-serve garlic cheese bread toasted in the oven until cheese is melted.

Garlic Herb Tortellini

Little morsels of pasta and vegetables deliciously saturated with garlic and herbs.

Package of fresh three-cheese tortellini	12 1/2 oz.	350 g
Boiling water	10 cups	2.5 L
Salt	1 1/4 tsp.	6 mL
Frozen California vegetable mix, thawed	1 1/2 cups	375 mL
Butter (not margarine)	3 tbsp.	50 mL
Chopped fresh chives	2 tbsp.	30 mL
Chopped fresh parsley	2 tbsp.	30 mL
Garlic cloves, minced	2	2
Pepper	1/8 tsp.	0.5 mL

Cook tortellini in boiling water and salt in large uncovered pot or Dutch oven for 6 minutes, stirring occasionally. Add vegetable mix. Cook for 3 to 4 minutes until vegetables are tender-crisp and tortellini is tender but firm. Drain. Return to same pot. Cover to keep warm.

Melt butter in large frying pan on medium. Add remaining 4 ingredients. Heat and stir for about 2 minutes until fragrant. Add to tortellini mixture. Toss well. Serves 4.

1 serving: 287 Calories; 16.4 g Total Fat (2.6 g Mono, 0.4 g Poly, 5.5 g Sat); 76 mg Cholesterol; 24 g Carbohydrate; 2 g Fibre; 12 g Protein; 331 mg Sodium

Make It A Meal with a salad of tomato slices and grated part-skim mozzarella cheese drizzled with balsamic vinaigrette and sprinkled with salt and pepper.

Rapid Rice Burritos

*A great way to use leftover rice. These will be a hit
with young and old alike.*

RAPID RICE FILLING

Cooked long grain white rice (about 1/2 cup, 125 mL, uncooked)	1 1/4 cups	300 mL
Can of red kidney beans, rinsed and drained	19 oz.	540 mL
Salsa	1/3 cup	75 mL
Thinly sliced green onion	1/4 cup	60 mL
Sour cream	3 tbsp.	50 mL
Diced jalapeño pepper (see Tip, page 23)	1	1
Dried cilantro or parsley flakes (or 2 tsp., 10 mL, chopped fresh), optional	1/2 tsp.	2 mL
Flour tortillas (9 inch, 22 cm, diameter)	8	8
Grated sharp Cheddar cheese	1 cup	250 mL

Rapid Rice Filling: Microwave cooked rice in medium bowl on high (100%) for about 1 1/2 minutes until warm.

Preheat electric grill for 5 minutes. Combine next 6 ingredients in large bowl. Add rice. Stir well. Makes about 3 cups (750 mL) filling.

Spoon about 1/3 cup (75 mL) filling across centre of 1 tortilla. Sprinkle about 2 tbsp. (30 mL) cheese over filling. Fold sides over filling. Roll up from bottom to enclose. Repeat with remaining tortillas, filling and cheese. Spray each burrito with cooking spray. Cook on greased grill (see Note) for about 3 minutes per side, turning 1/4 turn every 1 1/2 minutes, until grill marks appear and cheese is melted. Makes 8 burritos.

1 burrito: 284 Calories; 8.7 g Total Fat (2.8 g Mono, 1.4 g Poly, 4.1 g Sat); 18 mg Cholesterol; 40 g Carbohydrate; 4 g Fibre; 11 g Protein; 385 mg Sodium

Note: If preferred, place burritos on greased baking sheet. Bake in 400°F (205°C) oven for about 10 minutes, turning burritos at halftime, until golden and cheese is melted.

Make It A Meal with a salad of romaine lettuce, sliced tomatoes and chopped avocado tossed with a roasted red pepper dressing.

Dill Seafood Shell Salad

With a creamy dill dressing, this fresh,
light crab and pasta salad is definitely a winner!

Small shell pasta	1 1/2 cups	375 mL
Boiling water	10 cups	2.5 L
Salt	1 1/4 tsp.	6 mL
Frozen peas	1/2 cup	125 mL
Cans of crabmeat (6 oz., 170 g, each), drained, cartilage removed (or imitation), flaked	2	2
Chopped red pepper	1 cup	250 mL
Can of sliced water chestnuts, drained	8 oz.	227 mL
Sliced green onion	1/4 cup	60 mL
DILL DRESSING		
Sour cream	1/2 cup	125 mL
Salad dressing (or mayonnaise)	1/4 cup	60 mL
Milk	1 tbsp.	15 mL
Lemon juice	2 tsp.	10 mL
Dill weed (or 4 tsp., 20 mL, chopped fresh dill)	1 tsp.	5 mL
Worcestershire sauce	1/4 tsp.	1 mL
Salt	1/2 tsp.	2 mL

Cook pasta in boiling water and salt in large uncovered pot or Dutch oven for 8 minutes, stirring occasionally.

Add peas. Cook for 2 to 3 minutes until peas are tender-crisp and pasta is tender but firm. Drain. Rinse with cold water until cool. Drain well.

Put next 4 ingredients into large bowl. Stir. Add pasta mixture. Toss.

Dill Dressing: Combine all 7 ingredients in small bowl. Makes about 3/4 cup (175 mL) dressing. Drizzle over salad. Toss gently. Serves 4.

1 serving: 324 Calories; 13 g Total Fat (5.6 g Mono, 3 g Poly, 3.3 g Sat), 16 mg Cholesterol; 39 g Carbohydrate; 3 g Fibre; 13 g Protein; 714 mg Sodium

Make It A Meal with grilled or broiled shrimp skewers brushed with Italian dressing. Ready-made skewers can be purchased in your grocer's meat department and cooked according to package directions.

Warm Yammy Chicken Salad

Golden roasted yam nestles nicely in this rich, deep green salad.

Yam (or sweet potato), peeled, cut into 1/2 inch (12 mm) pieces	1 lb.	454 g
Salt, sprinkle		
Pepper, sprinkle		
Olive (or cooking) oil	1 tbsp.	15 mL
Boneless, skinless chicken breast halves, cut into 3/4 inch (2 cm) pieces	1 lb.	454 g
Fresh asparagus, trimmed of tough ends, cut into 1 inch (2.5 cm) pieces	1 lb.	454 g
Fresh spinach leaves, lightly packed	4 cups	1 L
PARMESAN DRESSING		
Grated Parmesan cheese	1/3 cup	75 mL
Olive (or cooking) oil	4 tbsp.	60 mL
Red wine vinegar	2 tbsp.	30 mL
Dried basil	1 1/2 tsp.	7 mL
Toasted pine nuts (see Tip, page 46), optional	3 tbsp.	50 mL

Preheat oven to 475°F (240°C). Spread yam evenly on greased baking sheet with sides. Spray with cooking spray. Sprinkle with salt and pepper. Bake for about 20 minutes, stirring once, until yam is tender and golden.

Meanwhile, heat olive oil in large frying pan on medium-high. Add chicken. Cook for about 4 minutes, stirring occasionally, until starting to brown. Add asparagus. Cook for about 5 minutes, stirring often, until asparagus is tender-crisp and chicken is no longer pink inside.

Put spinach into large bowl. Add chicken mixture and yam. Toss.

Parmesan Dressing: Combine first 4 ingredients in jar with tight-fitting lid. Shake well. Makes about 1/2 cup (125 mL) dressing. Drizzle over salad. Toss well.

Sprinkle with pine nuts. Serves 4.

1 serving: 480 Calories; 23 g Total Fat (14.4 g Mono, 2.2 g Poly, 4.7 g Sat); 73 mg Cholesterol; 36 g Carbohydrate; 7 g Fibre; 35 g Protein; 221 mg Sodium

Make It A Meal with whole grain crusty buns or warm focaccia bread.

Summer Pasta Salad

Refreshing lemon, parsley and tomato turn tuna and pasta into a cool salad for a warm day.

Fusilli (or other spiral) pasta (about 9 oz., 255 g)	3 cups	750 mL
Boiling water	12 cups	3 L
Salt	1 1/2 tsp.	7 mL
Diced tomato	1 cup	250 mL
Can of flaked tuna packed in water, drained	6 oz.	170 g
Chopped fresh parsley	1/3 cup	75 mL
Olive oil	1/4 cup	60 mL
Lemon juice	1/4 cup	60 mL
Salt	1/2 tsp.	2 mL
Pepper	1/4 tsp.	1 mL
Grated Parmesan cheese	1 tbsp.	15 mL
Pepper, sprinkle		

Cook pasta in boiling water and first amount of salt in large uncovered pot or Dutch oven for 8 to 10 minutes, stirring occasionally, until tender but firm. Drain. Rinse with cold water until cool. Drain well.

Meanwhile, combine next 7 ingredients in large bowl. Add pasta. Toss well.

Sprinkle with Parmesan cheese and pepper. Serves 4.

1 serving: 412 Calories; 17.1 g Total Fat (11.2 g Mono, 2.1 g Poly, 2.7 g Sat); 17 mg Cholesterol; 47 g Carbohydrate; 3 g Fibre; 18 g Protein; 481 mg Sodium

Make It A Meal with your favourite olives, sliced deli cheeses and crisp flatbread.

Paré Pointer

No one made a fool out of him—he's a do-it-yourself type.

Salmon Spinach Salad

Don't let the dressing fool you—it has just the right amount
of zing to complement salmon and spinach.

Chopped fresh green beans	1 cup	250 mL
Water	5 cups	1.25 L
Dill weed	1/2 tsp.	2 mL
Salt	1/2 tsp.	2 mL
Fresh (or frozen, thawed) salmon fillets, skin removed	1 lb.	454 g
Fresh spinach leaves, lightly packed	5 cups	1.25 L
Cherry tomatoes, halved	8 oz.	225 g
HORSERADISH DRESSING		
Cooking oil	3 tbsp.	50 mL
White wine vinegar	2 tbsp.	30 mL
Creamed horseradish	1 tbsp.	15 mL
Liquid honey	1 tbsp.	15 mL
Salt	1/4 tsp.	1 mL

Put green beans into small microwave-safe dish. Cover. Microwave on high (100%) for about 2 minutes until tender-crisp. Drain. Rinse with cold water until cool. Drain well. Set aside.

Measure next 3 ingredients into medium frying pan. Cover. Bring to a boil on medium-high.

Add salmon. Reduce heat to low. Cover. Simmer for about 7 minutes until fish flakes easily when tested with fork. Transfer salmon with slotted spoon to large plate. Discard liquid. Coarsely flake salmon with fork.

Put spinach and tomato into large bowl. Add flaked salmon. Toss gently. Add green beans. Toss.

Horseradish Dressing: Combine all 5 ingredients in jar with tight-fitting lid. Shake well. Makes about 1/2 cup (125 mL) dressing. Drizzle over salad. Toss gently. Serves 4.

(continued on next page)

1 serving: 309 Calories; 18.1 g Total Fat (8.5 g Mono, 6.2 g Poly, 1.9 g Sat); 62 mg Cholesterol; 13 g Carbohydrate; 3 g Fibre; 26 g Protein; 416 mg Sodium

Make It A Meal with frozen seasoned potato wedges cooked according to package directions.

Apple Chicken Salad

*A light salad the entire family will enjoy,
and a great way to use leftover chicken.*

Chopped or torn romaine lettuce, lightly packed	4 cups	1 L
Chopped cooked chicken	3 cups	750 mL
Medium cooking apples (such as McIntosh), with skin, cores removed, diced	2	2
Sliced celery	2/3 cup	150 mL
Toasted walnut pieces (see Tip, page 46)	1/3 cup	75 mL
CREAMY HONEY DRESSING		
Salad dressing (or mayonnaise)	1/4 cup	60 mL
Sour cream	2 tbsp.	30 mL
Lemon juice	2 tbsp.	30 mL
Liquid honey	1 tbsp.	15 mL
Salt, just a pinch		
Pepper, just a pinch		

Put first 5 ingredients into large bowl. Toss.

Creamy Honey Dressing: Combine all 6 ingredients in small bowl. Makes about 1/2 cup (125 mL) dressing. Drizzle over salad. Toss gently. Serves 6.

1 serving: 287 Calories; 15.2 g Total Fat (5.9 g Mono, 5.4 g Poly, 2.7 g Sat); 71 mg Cholesterol; 14 g Carbohydrate; 2 g Fibre; 24 g Protein; 148 mg Sodium

Make It A Meal with grilled cheese sandwiches and heat-and-serve cream of asparagus or broccoli soup.

Warm Spinach Lentil Salad

An earthy blend of spinach, roasted red pepper, lentils and creamy goat cheese.
Arugula may be used in place of spinach for a more peppery tasting salad.

Fresh spinach leaves, lightly packed	5 cups	1.25 L
Roasted red peppers, drained, blotted dry, cut into strips	1 cup	250 mL
Goat (chèvre) cheese, cut up	4 1/2 oz.	127 g
Cooking oil	2 tsp.	10 mL
Finely chopped red onion	1/2 cup	125 mL
Ground cumin	1/2 tsp.	2 mL
Ground coriander	1/2 tsp.	2 mL
Chili powder	1/2 tsp.	2 mL
Can of lentils, rinsed and drained	19 oz.	540 mL
LEMON HONEY VINAIGRETTE		
Lemon juice	3 tbsp.	50 mL
Olive (or cooking) oil	1 1/2 tbsp.	25 mL
Liquid honey	1 tbsp.	15 mL
Salt	1/4 tsp.	1 mL

Put spinach, red pepper and cheese into large bowl. Toss. Set aside.

Heat cooking oil in medium frying pan on medium. Add onion. Cook for 5 to 10 minutes, stirring often, until onion is softened.

Add next 3 ingredients. Heat and stir for about 1 minute until fragrant. Remove from heat.

Add lentils. Stir. Add to spinach mixture. Toss.

Lemon Honey Vinaigrette: Combine all 4 ingredients in jar with tight-fitting lid. Shake well. Makes about 1/3 cup (75 mL) vinaigrette. Drizzle over salad. Toss well. Serves 4.

1 serving: 320 Calories; 17.7 g Total Fat (7.4 g Mono, 1.6 g Poly, 7.5 g Sat); 25 mg Cholesterol; 28 g Carbohydrate; 6 g Fibre; 16 g Protein; 545 mg Sodium

Make It A Meal with ready-made hummus from your grocer's deli and crusty Italian bread.

Chorizo Orange Salad

*An eye-catching salad with a wide assortment
of flavours and textures. Sure to be a hit!*

Cooking oil	1 tsp.	5 mL
Chorizo sausages, cut into 1/4 inch (6 mm) slices	1 lb.	454 g
Chopped or torn romaine lettuce, lightly packed	6 cups	1.5 L
Medium oranges, chopped	2	2
Coarsely chopped toasted pecans (see Tip, page 46)	2/3 cup	150 mL
Roasted red peppers, drained, blotted dry, chopped	1/2 cup	125 mL
Ripe pitted whole olives	1/3 cup	75 mL
Thinly sliced red onion	1/3 cup	75 mL
GARLIC DRESSING		
Olive (or cooking) oil	1/4 cup	60 mL
White wine vinegar	2 tbsp.	30 mL
Garlic cloves, minced (or 1/2 tsp., 2 mL, powder)	2	2
Brown sugar, packed	2 tsp.	10 mL
Dried crushed chilies	1 tsp.	5 mL
Salt	1/8 tsp.	0.5 mL

Heat cooking oil in large frying pan on medium. Add sausage. Cook for about 15 minutes, stirring occasionally, until no longer pink. Transfer with slotted spoon to paper towels to drain.

Meanwhile, put next 6 ingredients into large bowl. Toss gently.

Garlic Dressing: Combine all 6 ingredients in jar with tight-fitting lid. Shake well. Makes about 1/2 cup (125 mL) dressing. Drizzle over salad. Add sausage. Toss well. Serves 6.

1 serving: 351 Calories; 29.6 g Total Fat (18 g Mono, 4.7 g Poly, 5.4 g Sat); 28 mg Cholesterol; 14 g Carbohydrate; 3 g Fibre; 10 g Protein; 433 mg Sodium

Make It A Meal with a warm focaccia loaf or heat-and-serve garlic bread.

Shrimp Caesar Salad

Traditional Caesar taste with a Tex-Mex twist.

Precooked bacon slices	4	4
Chopped or torn romaine lettuce, lightly packed	6 cups	1.5 L
Coarsely crushed tortilla chips	2 cups	500 mL
Grated Parmesan cheese	1/2 cup	125 mL
Frozen uncooked large shrimp (peeled, deveined), thawed	1 lb.	454 g
Salad dressing (or mayonnaise)	1/4 cup	60 mL
Lemon juice	1 tbsp.	15 mL
Chili powder	1 tsp.	5 mL
Cooking oil	2 tsp.	10 mL
ZESTY CAESAR DRESSING		
Caesar salad dressing	1/4 cup	60 mL
Lemon juice	1 tbsp.	15 mL
Pepper	1/4 tsp.	1 mL

Heat precooked bacon according to package directions until crisp. Crumble into extra-large bowl.

Add lettuce, tortilla chips and Parmesan cheese. Toss.

Measure next 4 ingredients into medium bowl. Stir until shrimp are coated.

Heat cooking oil in large frying pan on medium-high. Add shrimp mixture. Heat and stir for 2 to 3 minutes until shrimp turn pink. Add to salad.

Zesty Caesar Dressing: Combine all 3 ingredients in small bowl. Makes about 1/3 cup (75 mL) dressing. Drizzle over salad. Toss gently. Serves 4.

1 serving: 509 Calories; 32.8 g Total Fat (12.7 g Mono, 5.4 g Poly, 7.3 g Sat); 152 mg Cholesterol; 25 g Carbohydrate; 3 g Fibre; 29 g Protein; 924 mg Sodium

Make It A Meal with French bread slices spread with garlic butter and sprinkled with grated Cheddar or mozzarella cheese. Broil until cheese is melted.

Meatball Salad

Ready-made uncooked beef meatballs, available in the meat section
of many grocery stores, provide a quick answer to dinner.
Try them in this delicious warm salad.

Package of uncooked beef meatballs	1 lb.	454 g
Salt, sprinkle		
Pepper, sprinkle		
Chopped or torn romaine lettuce, lightly packed	6 cups	1.5 L
Diced part-skim mozzarella cheese	1 cup	250 mL
Thinly sliced yellow pepper	1 cup	250 mL
Cherry tomatoes, halved	8 oz.	225 g
PESTO DRESSING		
Basil pesto	1/4 cup	60 mL
White wine vinegar	2 tbsp.	30 mL
Olive (or cooking) oil	1 tbsp.	15 mL
Granulated sugar	1 tsp.	5 mL

Preheat broiler. Arrange meatballs in single layer on greased baking sheet with sides. Sprinkle with salt and pepper. Broil 6 inches (15 cm) from heat in oven for about 14 minutes, turning at halftime, until no longer pink inside. Remove with slotted spoon to paper towels to drain.

Put next 4 ingredients into extra-large bowl. Add meatballs.

Pesto Dressing: Combine all 4 ingredients in jar with tight-fitting lid. Shake well. Makes about 1/2 cup (125 mL) dressing. Drizzle over salad. Toss gently. Serves 4.

1 serving: 313 Calories; 14.2 g Total Fat (4.2 g Mono, 0.6 g Poly, 4.2 g Sat); 21 mg Cholesterol; 28 g Carbohydrate; 3 g Fibre; 19 g Protein; 469 mg Sodium

Pictured on page 107.

Make It A Meal by stuffing this salad into pita pockets to eat and run!

Paré Pointer
Anyone who claims to be too old to learn
anything new probably always was.

Couscous Pork Salad

Pork and raisins are a lovely combination in this filling salad.

Prepared chicken broth	1 1/4 cups	300 mL
Couscous	1 1/4 cups	300 mL
Dark raisins	1/3 cup	75 mL
Olive (or cooking) oil	1 tbsp.	15 mL
Boneless pork loin chops, trimmed of fat	1 lb.	454 g
Small zucchini (with peel), cut lengthwise into 1/4 inch (6 mm) slices	2	2
Salt, sprinkle		
Pepper, sprinkle		

ORANGE VINAIGRETTE

Olive (or cooking) oil	3 tbsp.	50 mL
Orange juice	3 tbsp.	50 mL
Grated orange zest	1 tsp.	5 mL
Ground cumin	1/2 tsp.	2 mL
Dried crushed chilies	1/4 tsp.	1 mL
Salt	1/4 tsp.	1 mL
Pepper	1/4 tsp.	1 mL

Preheat electric grill for 5 minutes or gas barbecue to medium (see Note). Measure broth into small saucepan. Bring to a boil on medium-high. Remove from heat.

Add couscous, raisins and olive oil. Stir. Cover. Let stand for 5 minutes. Fluff with fork. Transfer to large bowl.

Sprinkle pork chops and zucchini slices with salt and pepper. Cook chops on greased grill for 3 to 4 minutes per side until desired doneness. Cook zucchini slices on same greased grill for 2 to 3 minutes per side until tender-crisp. Chop zucchini and thinly slice pork. Add to couscous mixture. Toss.

Orange Vinaigrette: Combine all 7 ingredients in jar with tight-fitting lid. Shake well. Makes about 1/2 cup (125 mL) vinaigrette. Drizzle over salad. Toss well. Serves 4.

1 serving: 583 Calories; 20.6 g Total Fat (12.9 g Mono, 2.1 g Poly, 4.1 g Sat); 72 mg Cholesterol; 63 g Carbohydrate; 4 g Fibre; 36 g Protein; 492 mg Sodium

(continued on next page)

Note: Pork and zucchini may be broiled in oven. Place on greased broiler pan. Broil about 4 inches (10 cm) from heat in oven for about 4 minutes per side until desired doneness.

Make It A Meal with tomato wedges tossed with a balsamic vinaigrette.

Sweet Chicken Salad

An attractive salad full of sweet, tangy, good taste. This won't last long.

Chopped or torn romaine lettuce, lightly packed	7 cups	1.75 L
Chopped cooked chicken	3 cups	750 mL
Cherry tomatoes, halved	5 oz.	140 g
Dried cranberries	1/2 cup	125 mL
Crumbled feta cheese (about 2 1/2 oz., 70 g)	1/2 cup	125 mL
Thinly sliced red onion	1/4 cup	60 mL
Toasted sliced natural almonds (see Tip, page 46)	3 tbsp.	50 mL
POPPY SEED DRESSING		
Cooking oil	3 tbsp.	50 mL
Balsamic vinegar	2 tbsp.	30 mL
Granulated sugar	1 tbsp.	15 mL
Poppy seeds	2 tsp.	10 mL
Worcestershire sauce	1/2 tsp.	2 mL
Pepper, just a pinch		

Put first 7 ingredients into large bowl. Toss.

Poppy Seed Dressing: Combine all 6 ingredients in jar with tight-fitting lid. Shake well. Makes about 1/3 cup (75 mL) dressing. Drizzle over salad. Toss well. Serves 6.

1 serving: 308 Calories; 17.8 g Total Fat (7.9 g Mono, 4.2 g Poly, 4.3 g Sat); 79 mg Cholesterol; 11 g Carbohydrate; 3 g Fibre; 26 g Protein; 231 mg Sodium

Make It A Meal with thick bread slices spread with a mixture of margarine or butter, Parmesan cheese, dried oregano and basil. Broil until toasted.

Chickpea Ham Salad

You can easily toss this colourful salad together when there's no time to cook.

Chopped tomato	2 1/2 cups	625 mL
Can of chickpeas (garbanzo beans), rinsed and drained	19 oz.	540 mL
Chopped English cucumber (with peel)	1 1/4 cups	300 mL
Chopped green pepper	1 cup	250 mL
Chopped deli ham	1 1/3 cups	325 mL
Thinly sliced red onion	1/2 cup	125 mL
LEMON GARLIC DRESSING		
Olive (or cooking) oil	3 tbsp.	50 mL
Lemon juice	3 tbsp.	50 mL
Parsley flakes	1 1/2 tsp.	7 mL
Garlic clove, minced (or 1/4 tsp., 1 mL, powder)	1	1
Granulated sugar	1/2 tsp.	2 mL
Salt	1/4 tsp.	1 mL

Put first 6 ingredients into extra-large bowl. Toss gently.

Lemon Garlic Dressing: Combine all 6 ingredients in jar with tight-fitting lid. Shake well. Makes about 1/3 cup (75 mL) dressing. Drizzle over salad. Toss gently. Serves 4.

1 serving: 338 Calories; 18.2 g Total Fat (10.8 g Mono, 2.4 g Poly, 3.5 g Sat); 32 mg Cholesterol; 29 g Carbohydrate; 5 g Fibre; 17 g Protein; 1043 mg Sodium

Pictured on page 107.

Make It A Meal with focaccia bread sprinkled fresh herbs and heated in the oven.

1. Meatball Salad, page 103
2. Chickpea Ham Salad, above

Mandarin Shrimp Salad

*Mild creamy dressing envelops a delightful combination of shrimp,
lettuce, radish and orange. An adventure for your taste buds!*

Frozen cooked large shrimp (peeled, deveined), thawed	1 lb.	454 g
Can of mandarin orange segments, drained	10 oz.	284 mL
Bag of salad greens	10 oz.	284 mL
Ripe large avocado, diced	1	1
Radishes, quartered	6	6
ZESTY RANCH DRESSING		
Ranch-style dressing	1/4 cup	60 mL
Lime juice	1 tbsp.	15 mL
Granulated sugar	1 tsp.	5 mL
Pepper	1/4 tsp.	1 mL

Put first 5 ingredients into extra-large bowl. Toss gently.

Zesty Ranch Dressing: Combine all 4 ingredients in small bowl. Makes
about 1/4 cup (60 mL) dressing. Drizzle over salad. Toss gently. Serves 4.

*1 serving: 403 Calories; 17.8 g Total Fat (9.2 g Mono, 4.4 g Poly, 2.4 g Sat); 199 mg Cholesterol;
34 g Carbohydrate; 11 g Fibre; 34 g Protein; 527 mg Sodium*

Pictured on page 126.

Make It A Meal with pita bread wedges toasted in the oven.

1. One-Dish Saucy Spaghetti,
   page 112
2. Turkey Sausage Pasta, page 110

Props courtesy of: Casa Bugatti
                    Danesco Inc.

Turkey Sausage Pasta

A savoury dish, dressed for dinner in bow ties. Quick, easy and delicious.

Medium bow (or other medium-sized) pasta (about 6 1/2 oz., 184 g)	3 cups	750 mL
Boiling water	8 cups	2 L
Salt	1 tsp.	5 mL
Cooking oil	2 tsp.	10 mL
Thinly sliced red pepper	1 cup	250 mL
Sliced red onion	3/4 cup	175 mL
Turkey sausages, casings removed, chopped	3/4 lb.	340 g
Basil pesto	3 tbsp.	50 mL
Grated Parmesan cheese	2 tbsp.	30 mL

Cook pasta in boiling water and salt in large uncovered pot or Dutch oven for 10 to 12 minutes, stirring occasionally, until tender but firm. Drain. Return to same pot. Cover to keep warm.

Meanwhile, heat cooking oil in large frying pan on medium. Add red pepper and onion. Cook for about 5 minutes, stirring often, until onion starts to soften.

Add sausage. Cook for about 8 minutes, stirring occasionally, until sausage is no longer pink and onion is softened.

Add pesto. Stir. Add to pasta. Toss well. Remove to large serving dish.

Sprinkle with Parmesan cheese. Serves 4.

1 serving: 452 Calories; 14.6 g Total Fat (4.3 g Mono, 1.5 g Poly, 1.4 g Sat); 2 mg Cholesterol; 57 g Carbohydrate; 2 g Fibre; 25 g Protein; 855 mg Sodium

Pictured on page 108.

Make It A Meal with portobello mushroom slices and tomato halves brushed with a balsamic vinaigrette and sprinkled with salt and pepper. Broil in oven on an ungreased baking sheet for about 5 minutes until tender.

Beef Tortellini

A one-dish meal for the whole family.
Tasty tortellini topped with tomato and cheese is sure to please!

Package of fresh beef tortellini	12 1/2 oz.	350 g
Boiling water	10 cups	2.5 L
Salt	1 1/4 tsp.	6 mL
Cooking oil	1 tbsp.	15 mL
Chopped red pepper	1 cup	250 mL
Chopped cooked ham	1/2 cup	125 mL
Jar of pasta sauce (your choice)	16 oz.	500 mL
Dried crushed chilies	1/2 tsp.	2 mL
Medium tomato, thinly sliced	1	1
Grated sharp Cheddar cheese	1/2 cup	125 mL
Grated Parmesan cheese	1/3 cup	75 mL

Cook tortellini in boiling water and salt in large uncovered pot or Dutch oven for about 6 minutes, stirring occasionally, until tender but firm. Drain. Return to same pot. Cover to keep warm.

Meanwhile, heat cooking oil in large frying pan on medium. Add red pepper and ham. Cook for about 5 minutes, stirring occasionally, until red pepper is tender-crisp.

Add pasta sauce and chilies. Stir. Bring to a boil. Boil gently, uncovered, for about 5 minutes, stirring occasionally, until slightly thickened.

Preheat broiler. Add tortellini to sauce. Heat and stir for about 1 minute until heated through. Spread evenly in greased 9 x 9 inch (22 x 22 cm) pan. Arrange tomato slices, slightly overlapping, on top of tortellini mixture.

Sprinkle with both cheeses. Broil 6 inches (15 cm) from heat in oven for about 5 minutes until cheese is melted and golden. Serves 4.

1 serving: 508 Calories; 26.7 g Total Fat (8.3 g Mono, 3.3 g Poly, 6.6 g Sat); 86 mg Cholesterol; 44 g Carbohydrate; 3 g Fibre; 25 g Protein; 1415 mg Sodium

Make It A Meal with hot green beans tossed with margarine or butter and sprinkled with salt and pepper.

One-Dish Saucy Spaghetti

The family will enjoy this—and there's only one dish to clean! A nice balance
of herbs, sausage and mushrooms in a tangy tomato sauce.

Cooking oil	1 tsp.	5 mL
Hot Italian sausages, cut into 1 inch (2.5 cm) pieces	1/2 lb.	225 g
Cooking oil	1/2 tsp.	2 mL
Lean ground beef	1/2 lb.	225 g
Chopped onion	1/2 cup	125 mL
Garlic clove, minced (or 1/4 tsp., 1 mL, powder)	1	1
Can of diced tomatoes (with juice)	14 oz.	398 mL
Can of mushroom stems and pieces (with liquid)	10 oz.	284 mL
Water	1 cup	250 mL
Can of tomato sauce	7 1/2 oz.	213 mL
Dried whole oregano	1/2 tsp.	2 mL
Dried thyme	1/2 tsp.	2 mL
Dried basil	1/2 tsp.	2 mL
Salt	1/4 tsp.	1 mL
Pepper	1/4 tsp.	1 mL
Spaghetti, broken up	6 oz.	170 g

Heat first amount of cooking oil in large frying pan on medium. Add sausage. Cook for about 5 minutes, stirring occasionally, until browned. Transfer with slotted spoon to paper towels to drain. Set aside. Discard drippings.

Heat second amount of cooking oil in same large frying pan on medium-high. Add ground beef, onion and garlic. Scramble-fry for 5 to 10 minutes until beef is no longer pink and onion is softened. Drain.

Add sausage and next 9 ingredients. Stir. Bring to a boil.

(continued on next page)

Pasta

Add spaghetti. Stir. Reduce heat to medium-low. Cover. Simmer for
8 to 10 minutes, stirring occasionally, until spaghetti is tender but firm.
Remove cover. Simmer for 1 to 2 minutes until sauce is thickened.
Serves 4.

*1 serving: 400 Calories; 14.4 g Total Fat (6.4 g Mono, 2 g Poly, 4.5 g Sat); 50 mg Cholesterol;
45 g Carbohydrate; 4 g Fibre; 24 g Protein; 1065 mg Sodium*

Pictured on page 108.

Make It A Meal with a salad of lettuce, red onion and toasted pecan
pieces tossed with a raspberry vinaigrette. Serve with toasted and buttered
French bread slices.

Paré Pointer
Police were called when fish were being battered.

Chicken And Bacon Spaghetti

Asiago cheese adds a mild, nutty flavour to this creamy spaghetti dinner.
A delicious way to use leftover chicken.

Spaghetti	9 oz.	255 g
Boiling water	10 cups	2.5 L
Salt	1 1/4 tsp.	6 mL
Bacon slices, diced	8	8
Chopped green onion	1 cup	250 mL
All-purpose flour	1 tbsp.	15 mL
Can of skim evaporated milk	6 oz.	170 mL
Milk	1 1/4 cups	300 mL
Ground nutmeg	1/8 tsp.	0.5 mL
Pepper	1/4 tsp.	1 mL
Chopped cooked chicken	2 1/2 cups	625 mL
Frozen peas	1 cup	250 mL
Grated Asiago (or Parmesan) cheese	3/4 cup	175 mL
Freshly ground pepper, for garnish		

Cook spaghetti in boiling water and salt in large uncovered pot or Dutch oven for 8 to 10 minutes, stirring occasionally, until tender but firm. Drain. Return to same pot. Cover to keep warm.

Meanwhile, cook bacon in large saucepan on medium-high for about 5 minutes until almost crisp. Add onion. Cook for about 1 minute, stirring occasionally, until onion turns bright green.

Add flour. Heat and stir for 1 minute. Slowly add evaporated milk, stirring constantly until smooth. Add milk, nutmeg and pepper. Heat and stir for about 3 minutes until boiling and thickened.

Add chicken and peas. Stir. Reduce heat to medium-low. Simmer for about 5 minutes, stirring occasionally, until heated through. Add to spaghetti.

Add cheese. Toss well. Remove to large serving dish. Garnish with pepper. Serves 4.

1 serving: 673 Calories; 24.2 g Total Fat (8.5 g Mono, 3.1 g Poly, 10.5 g Sat); 131 mg Cholesterol; 60 g Carbohydrate; 4 g Fibre; 51 g Protein; 515 mg Sodium

(continued on next page)

Make It A Meal with a salad of chopped tomato, onion and green pepper sprinkled with dried whole oregano, salt and pepper. Drizzle with olive oil and balsamic vinegar.

Nutty Asparagus Linguine

Basil pesto, sun-dried tomatoes and pecans accent asparagus perfectly—a memorable dish!

Linguine pasta	5 1/4 oz.	150 g
Boiling water	6 cups	1.5 L
Salt	3/4 tsp.	4 mL
Fresh asparagus, trimmed of tough ends, cut into 1 inch (2.5 cm) pieces	1 lb.	454 g
Water		
PESTO DRESSING		
Olive oil	1/3 cup	75 mL
Basil pesto	1/4 cup	60 mL
White wine vinegar	2 tbsp.	30 mL
Sun-dried tomatoes in oil, drained and sliced	1/2 cup	125 mL
Toasted pecan pieces (see Tip, page 46)	1/2 cup	125 mL

Cook pasta in boiling water and salt in large uncovered pot or Dutch oven for 10 to 12 minutes, stirring occasionally, until tender but firm. Drain. Return to same pot. Cover to keep warm.

Cook asparagus in water in medium saucepan until tender-crisp. Drain. Meanwhile, prepare Pesto Dressing.

Pesto Dressing: Combine olive oil, pesto and vinegar in jar with tight-fitting lid. Shake well. Makes about 1/2 cup (125 mL) dressing. Drizzle over pasta.

Add asparagus, sun-dried tomatoes and pecans. Toss well. Serves 4.

1 serving: 498 Calories; 36 g Total Fat (24.7 g Mono, 5 g Poly, 4.4 g Sat); 0 mg Cholesterol; 39 g Carbohydrate; 3 g Fibre; 9 g Protein; 44 mg Sodium

Make It A Meal with grilled or broiled chicken thighs or lamb chops brushed with a mixture of lemon juice, olive oil, minced garlic and freshly ground pepper.

Linguine Carbonara

*Smoky bacon and sharp Romano cheese give this simple pasta
a bold, satisfying flavour.*

Linguine pasta	12 1/2 oz.	354 g
Boiling water	10 cups	2.5 L
Salt	1 1/4 tsp.	6 mL
Bacon slices, diced	6	6
Sliced fresh white mushrooms	1 cup	250 mL
Chopped onion	1/2 cup	125 mL
Garlic clove, minced (or 1/4 tsp., 1 mL, powder)	1	1
Large eggs	4	4
Grated Romano (or Parmesan) cheese	1/2 cup	125 mL
Chopped fresh parsley	2 tbsp.	30 mL
Pepper	1/2 tsp.	2 mL

Cook pasta in boiling water and salt in large uncovered pot or Dutch oven for 8 to 10 minutes, stirring occasionally, until tender but firm. Drain, reserving 1 cup (250 mL) cooking water. Set aside. Return pasta to same pot. Cover to keep warm.

Meanwhile, cook bacon in large frying pan on medium-high until almost crisp.

Add mushrooms, onion and garlic. Cook for 5 to 10 minutes, stirring often, until bacon is crisp and onion is softened.

Beat remaining 4 ingredients with whisk in medium bowl until well combined. Add pasta to bacon mixture. Add egg mixture. Heat and toss on medium-low for 1 to 2 minutes until egg mixture thickens and pasta is coated. If sauce is too thick, add reserved cooking water 1 tbsp. (15 mL) at a time, tossing after each addition, until desired consistency. Serves 4.

1 serving: 533 Calories; 15.2 g Total Fat (5.5 g Mono, 2 g Poly, 5.9 g Sat); 234 mg Cholesterol; 70 g Carbohydrate; 3 g Fibre; 27 g Protein; 469 mg Sodium

Make It A Meal with a Caesar salad kit (available in your grocer's produce department). Serve with bread sticks.

Chicken Herb Linguine

Lightly coated linguine with a chili heat that lingers.
A great way to use leftover chicken.

Linguine pasta	7 oz.	200 g
Boiling water	10 cups	2.5 L
Salt	1 1/4 tsp.	6 mL
Olive (or cooking) oil	2 tbsp.	30 mL
Garlic cloves, minced	2	2
Chopped cooked chicken	2 cups	500 mL
Chili paste (sambal oelek)	2 tsp.	10 mL
Prepared chicken broth	1/4 cup	60 mL
Chopped fresh basil	1/4 cup	60 mL
Chopped fresh parsley	1/4 cup	60 mL
Crumbled feta cheese (about 1 1/4 oz., 35 g), optional	1/4 cup	60 mL
Salt, sprinkle		

Cook pasta in boiling water and first amount of salt in large uncovered pot or Dutch oven for 10 to 12 minutes, stirring occasionally, until tender but firm. Drain. Return to same pot. Cover to keep warm.

Meanwhile, heat olive oil in medium frying pan on medium. Add garlic. Heat and stir for 1 to 2 minutes until fragrant.

Add chicken and chili paste. Heat and stir for about 5 minutes until chicken is heated through. Add to pasta. Cover to keep warm.

Combine next 3 ingredients in same medium frying pan. Bring to a boil. Add to pasta. Toss well. Remove to large serving dish.

Sprinkle with cheese and second amount of salt. Serves 4.

1 serving: 396 Calories; 13.4 g Total Fat (7.2 g Mono, 2.2 g Poly, 2.6 g Sat); 67 mg Cholesterol; 38 g Carbohydrate; 1 g Fibre; 29 g Protein; 123 mg Sodium

Make It A Meal with a salad of fresh spinach leaves, dried cranberries, thinly sliced red onion and halved cherry tomatoes drizzled with a roasted red pepper dressing or balsamic vinaigrette.

Shanghai Noodle Bowl

Colourful and loaded with vegetables. Peanut sauce adds
a gentle heat to this one-dish meal. For a perfect stir-fry,
prepare all the vegetables before you start cooking.

Water	1 tbsp.	15 mL
Cornstarch	1 tbsp.	15 mL
Cooking oil	2 tsp.	10 mL
Boneless, skinless chicken breast halves, cut into 1/4 inch (6 mm) slices	1 lb.	454 g
Package of fresh Shanghai noodles	1 lb.	454 g
Prepared chicken broth	1 cup	250 mL
Cooking oil	2 tsp.	10 mL
Whole baby bok choy, quartered lengthwise	4	4
Baby carrots, halved lengthwise	1 cup	250 mL
Coarsely chopped red pepper	1 cup	250 mL
Can of cut baby corn, drained	14 oz.	398 mL
Can of sliced mushrooms, drained	10 oz.	284 mL
Snow peas, trimmed	1 cup	250 mL
Can of sliced water chestnuts, drained	8 oz.	227 mL
Green onions, cut into 1 inch (2.5 cm) pieces	8	8
Bottle of Szechuan peanut sauce	12 1/2 oz.	350 mL
Chopped fresh cilantro or parsley (optional)	1 tbsp.	15 mL

Stir water into cornstarch in small cup until smooth. Set aside.

Heat wok or large frying pan on medium-high until very hot. Add first amount of cooking oil. Add chicken. Stir-fry for 5 to 10 minutes until no longer pink inside. Transfer to medium bowl. Cover to keep warm.

Meanwhile, combine noodles and broth in large microwave-safe dish. Cover with plastic wrap. Microwave on high (100%) for about 1 minute until noodles are heated through. Set aside.

(continued on next page)

Heat second amount of cooking oil in same wok on medium-high. Add bok choy, carrot and red pepper. Stir-fry for 2 minutes.

Add next 5 ingredients. Stir-fry for 2 minutes. Add noodles with broth. Toss well. Cover. Cook on high for about 2 minutes until vegetables are tender-crisp.

Stir cornstarch mixture. Add to noodle mixture. Add chicken and peanut sauce. Heat and stir for about 2 minutes until sauce is boiling and thickened. Remove to large serving bowl.

Sprinkle with cilantro. Serves 4.

1 serving: 800 Calories; 35.3 g Total Fat (14.4 g Mono, 9.1 g Poly, 9.3 g Sat); 66 mg Cholesterol; 80 g Carbohydrate; 10 g Fibre; 51 g Protein; 2056 mg Sodium

Make It A Meal with green tea and fortune cookies.

Paré Pointer

Some days she wakes up grumpy and some days she lets him sleep.

Vegetable Couscous

Golden couscous accented with tender vegetables
makes a delicious side dish for seafood.

Prepared chicken (or vegetable) broth	1 cup	250 mL
Couscous	1 cup	250 mL
Olive (or cooking) oil	2 tsp.	10 mL
Toasted slivered almonds (see Tip, page 46)	1/4 cup	60 mL
Liquid honey	1 tbsp.	15 mL
Parsley flakes (or about 3 tbsp., 50 mL, chopped fresh parsley)	2 tsp.	10 mL
Hard margarine (or butter)	1 tbsp.	15 mL
Thinly sliced carrot	1/2 cup	125 mL
Chopped zucchini (with peel)	2 cups	500 mL
Sliced green onion	1/2 cup	125 mL
Frozen peas	1/2 cup	125 mL
Salt	1/2 tsp.	2 mL

Heat broth in covered medium saucepan on high until boiling. Remove from heat. Add couscous and olive oil. Stir. Cover. Let stand for 5 minutes. Fluff with fork.

Add almonds, honey and parsley. Stir well. Cover to keep warm.

Melt margarine in large frying pan on medium-high. Add carrot. Heat and stir for about 4 minutes until starting to brown.

Add zucchini, onion, peas and salt. Heat and stir for about 4 minutes until zucchini is tender-crisp. Add to couscous mixture. Toss well. Serves 4.

1 serving: 344 Calories; 10.6 g Total Fat (6.7 g Mono, 1.7 g Poly, 1.5 g Sat); 0 mg Cholesterol; 52 g Carbohydrate; 5 g Fibre; 12 g Protein; 581 mg Sodium

Make It A Meal with salmon fillets poached in a mixture of salted water, dry white (or alcohol-free) wine, pepper and a bay leaf.

Sesame-Glazed Vegetables

*Crisp and colourful vegetable medley is an inviting side dish
to serve with just about anything.*

Cauliflower florets	2 cups	500 mL
Sliced carrot	2 cups	500 mL
Water		
Sugar snap peas, trimmed	2 cups	500 mL
Hard margarine (or butter)	1 tbsp.	15 mL
Liquid honey	1 tbsp.	15 mL
Sesame oil, for flavour	1/2 tsp.	2 mL
Dried thyme (or 1 tsp., 5 mL, chopped fresh thyme leaves)	1/4 tsp.	1 mL
Salt	1/4 tsp.	1 mL
Toasted sesame seeds (see Tip, page 46)	2 tsp.	10 mL

Cook cauliflower and carrot in water in large saucepan until starting to soften. Add peas. Cover. Cook until vegetables are tender-crisp. Drain.

Heat next 5 ingredients in large frying pan on low, stirring occasionally, until margarine is melted.

Add vegetables and sesame seeds. Stir until vegetables are coated. Serves 6.

1 serving: 93 Calories; 3.1 g Total Fat (1.6 g Mono, 0.7 g Poly, 0.6 g Sat); 0 mg Cholesterol; 15 g Carbohydrate; 3 g Fibre; 3 g Protein; 171 mg Sodium

Pictured on page 125.

Make It A Meal with microwave "baked" potatoes and grilled or broiled beef steaks.

Paré Pointer

Being thrifty is great—more ancestors should have practiced it.

Eggplant In Tomato Sauce

A zesty Italian-style side dish to serve with chicken.

Olive (or cooking) oil	1 tbsp.	15 mL
Cubed eggplant (with skin)	2 cups	500 mL
Chopped red onion	1 cup	250 mL
Chopped red pepper	1 cup	250 mL
Garlic cloves, minced (or 1/2 tsp., 2 mL, powder)	2	2
Can of diced tomatoes (with juice)	14 oz.	398 mL
Sweet chili sauce	1 tbsp.	15 mL
Balsamic vinegar	1 tbsp.	15 mL
Parsley flakes (or 2 tbsp., 30 mL, chopped fresh parsley)	1 1/2 tsp.	7 mL
Salt	1/2 tsp.	2 mL

Heat olive oil in large frying pan on medium. Add next 4 ingredients. Stir. Cook for about 5 minutes, stirring often, until eggplant is golden.

Add remaining 5 ingredients. Stir. Boil gently, uncovered, for about 4 minutes, stirring occasionally, until sauce is slightly thickened. Serves 4.

1 serving: 96 Calories; 3.9 g Total Fat (2.6 g Mono, 0.5 g Poly, 0.5 g Sat); 0 mg Cholesterol; 15 g Carbohydrate; 3 g Fibre; 2 g Protein; 523 mg Sodium

Pictured on page 125.

Make It A Meal with grilled or broiled boneless, skinless chicken thighs or breast halves sprinkled with Italian-style herbs.

Paré Pointer

What do you call cheese that isn't yours? Nacho cheese!

Potato And Pea Curry

Rich, creamy, coconut curry sauce highlights potato
in this just-a-little-different side dish.

Chopped peeled potato	3 cups	750 mL
Cooking oil	1 tbsp.	15 mL
Chopped onion	1 cup	250 mL
Mild curry paste	2 tbsp.	30 mL
All-purpose flour	2 tsp.	10 mL
Can of coconut milk	14 oz.	398 mL
Frozen peas	1 1/2 cups	375 mL
Frozen cut green beans	1 1/2 cups	375 mL
Water	1/4 cup	60 mL
Dried mint leaves (or 2 tbsp., 30 mL, chopped fresh), optional	1 1/2 tsp.	7 mL
Salt	1/2 tsp.	2 mL

Microwave potato in covered microwave-safe dish on high (100%) for about 8 minutes until tender. Drain liquid.

Meanwhile, heat cooking oil in large frying pan on medium. Add onion and curry paste. Cook for 5 to 10 minutes, stirring often, until onion is softened.

Add flour. Heat and stir for 1 minute.

Add potato and remaining 6 ingredients. Stir. Bring to a boil on medium-high. Reduce heat to medium. Simmer, uncovered, for about 5 minutes until sauce is boiling and thickened and green beans are tender-crisp. Serves 4.

1 serving: 423 Calories; 27 g Total Fat (4.3 g Mono, 2.2 g Poly, 18.5 g Sat); 0 mg Cholesterol; 42 g Carbohydrate; 6 g Fibre; 9 g Protein; 384 mg Sodium

Make It A Meal with grilled or broiled lamb chops or pork chops brushed with mango chutney.

Horseradish Potatoes

Creamy mashed potatoes with just a hint of horseradish
go great with beef or your favourite white fish.

Potatoes, peeled and quartered	2 lbs.	900 g
Water		
Salt	1/2 tsp.	2 mL
Finely chopped green onion	1/3 cup	75 mL
Sour cream	2 tbsp.	30 mL
Hard margarine (or butter)	1 tbsp.	15 mL
Creamed horseradish	1 tbsp.	15 mL
Salt, sprinkle		
Pepper	1/4 tsp.	1 mL

Cook potato in water and salt in large saucepan until tender. Drain. Return to same saucepan.

Combine remaining 6 ingredients in small bowl. Add to potato. Mash well. Serves 4.

1 serving: 200 Calories; 4.2 g Total Fat (2.2 g Mono, 0.4 g Poly, 1.3 g Sat); 3 mg Cholesterol; 37 g Carbohydrate; 3 g Fibre; 5 g Protein; 54 mg Sodium

Make It A Meal with grilled or broiled steak or fish. Serve with steamed asparagus spears or green beans dotted with herb and garlic spreadable cream cheese.

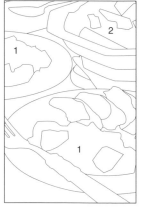

1. Eggplant In Tomato Sauce, page 122
2. Sesame-Glazed Vegetables, page 121

Props courtesy of: Casa Bugatti
Cherison Enterprises Inc.
Emile Henry

Two-Step Salad

Two easy steps and you're done! A variety of colours and textures make this an interesting salad to serve.

Can of mixed beans, rinsed and drained	19 oz.	540 mL
Can of artichoke hearts, drained and quartered	14 oz.	398 mL
Diced tomato	1 cup	250 mL
Grated sharp Cheddar cheese	1 cup	250 mL
Sliced green onion	2 tbsp.	30 mL
Italian dressing	1/4 cup	60 mL

Put first 5 ingredients into large bowl. Toss.

Drizzle with dressing. Toss well. Serves 6.

1 serving: 260 Calories; 14.5 g Total Fat (6 g Mono, 2.9 g Poly, 4.8 g Sat); 28 mg Cholesterol; 22 g Carbohydrate; 6 g Fibre; 12 g Protein; 480 mg Sodium

Make It A Meal with grilled or broiled lamb chops brushed with Italian dressing. Serve with warm crusty buns.

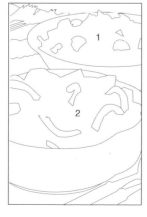

1. Mandarin Shrimp Salad, page 109
2. Cucumber And Potato Salad, page 128

Props courtesy of: Cherison Enterprises Inc.
Corelle®

Cucumber And Potato Salad

Refreshing, crunchy cucumber, tender baby potatoes and a sweet,
creamy dressing. This salad will have them asking for more!

Red baby potatoes, halved	1 lb.	454 g
Water		
Salt	1/2 tsp.	2 mL
English cucumber (with peel), halved lengthwise and sliced	1	1
Thinly sliced red pepper	1/2 cup	125 mL
Thinly sliced red onion	1/4 cup	60 mL
Toasted sesame seeds (see Tip, page 46)	1 tbsp.	15 mL
SOUR CREAM DRESSING		
Mayonnaise	1/4 cup	60 mL
Sour cream	1/4 cup	60 mL
Liquid honey	1 tbsp.	15 mL
Salt	1/4 tsp.	1 mL
Pepper	1/4 tsp.	1 mL

Cook potatoes in water and salt in large saucepan until just tender. Drain. Rinse with cold water until cool. Drain well.

Put next 4 ingredients into large bowl. Toss. Add potatoes.

Sour Cream Dressing: Combine all 5 ingredients in small bowl. Makes about 1/2 cup (125 mL) dressing. Add to potato mixture. Toss gently. Serves 4.

1 serving: 265 Calories; 15.3 g Total Fat (7.6 g Mono, 4.6 g Poly, 2.7 g Sat); 15 mg Cholesterol; 29 g Carbohydrate; 3 g Fibre; 4 g Protein; 242 mg Sodium

Pictured on page 126.

Make It A Meal with grilled or broiled chicken or turkey sausages. Serve with steamed broccoli florets sprinkled with toasted sunflower seeds.

Cabbage Noodle Salad

An attractive salad with a flavourful dressing that's just a bit different.
Lots of satisfying crunch, too!

Package of rice stick noodles	9 oz.	250 g
Boiling water		
Chopped English cucumber (with peel)	3 cups	750 mL
Shredded red cabbage, lightly packed	3 cups	750 mL
Chopped unsalted peanuts	1 1/3 cups	325 mL
Chopped fresh basil	1/2 cup	125 mL
PEANUT GARLIC SAUCE		
Peanut (or cooking) oil	2/3 cup	150 mL
Brown sugar, packed	1/3 cup	75 mL
Lime juice	1/3 cup	75 mL
Soy sauce	1/4 cup	60 mL
Garlic cloves, minced (or 1/2 tsp., 2 mL, powder)	2	2

Place noodles in large bowl. Add enough boiling water to cover. Let stand for about 10 minutes until softened. Drain. Rinse with cold water until cool. Drain well. Return to same bowl.

Add next 4 ingredients. Toss.

Peanut Garlic Sauce: Combine all 5 ingredients in jar with tight-fitting lid. Shake well. Makes about 1 1/2 cups (375 mL) sauce. Drizzle over noodle mixture. Toss well. Serves 6.

1 serving: 672 Calories; 43 g Total Fat (20.2 g Mono, 13.6 g Poly, 6.7 g Sat); 0 mg Cholesterol; 64 g Carbohydrate; 5 g Fibre; 13 g Protein; 748 mg Sodium

Make It A Meal with grilled or broiled chicken, beef or pork satay skewers and slices of fresh or canned pineapple.

Paré Pointer
A chess player gets happy when he takes a knight off.

Lively Greek Salad

Tangy Herb Dressing enhances traditional
Greek flavours in this crisp, tasty salad. So easy to make.

Chopped or torn romaine lettuce, lightly packed	6 cups	1.5 L
Medium English cucumber (with peel), quartered lengthwise and cut into 1 inch (2.5 cm) pieces	1	1
Chopped green pepper	1 cup	250 mL
Can of sliced ripe olives, drained	4 1/2 oz.	125 mL
TANGY HERB DRESSING		
Red wine vinegar	3 tbsp.	50 mL
Cooking oil	2 tbsp.	30 mL
Dried whole oregano	1/2 tsp.	2 mL
Dried basil	1/4 tsp.	1 mL
Pepper	1/4 tsp.	1 mL
Garlic powder	1/4 tsp.	1 mL
Cayenne pepper	1/4 tsp.	1 mL
Crumbled feta cheese (about 2 1/2 oz., 70 g)	1/2 cup	125 mL
Thinly sliced red onion	1/4 cup	60 mL
Medium tomatoes, each cut into 8 wedges	2	2

Put first 4 ingredients into large bowl. Toss.

Tangy Herb Dressing: Combine first 7 ingredients in jar with tight-fitting lid. Shake well. Makes about 1/4 cup (60 mL) dressing. Drizzle over salad. Toss well.

Add remaining 3 ingredients. Toss gently. Serves 6.

1 serving: 139 Calories; 10.2 g Total Fat (5.1 g Mono, 1.8 g Poly, 2.7 g Sat); 12 mg Cholesterol; 10 g Carbohydrate; 3 g Fibre; 4 g Protein; 348 mg Sodium

Make It A Meal with ready-made roasted chicken from your grocer's deli and warm pita bread.

Pea And Pickle Salad

A hearty salad to serve instead of potatoes.
A great way to use leftover hard-cooked eggs, too!

Large eggs	2	2
Cold water		
Fresh (or frozen, thawed) peas	2 cups	500 mL
Water		
Diced medium Cheddar cheese	1 cup	250 mL
Chopped celery	1/2 cup	125 mL
Chopped gherkins (or sweet pickles)	1/2 cup	125 mL
Green onions, chopped	2	2
SWEET AND CREAMY DRESSING		
Salad dressing (or mayonnaise)	6 tbsp.	100 mL
Milk	1 tbsp.	15 mL
Granulated sugar	1 1/2 tsp.	7 mL

Place eggs in small saucepan. Add cold water until about 1 inch (2.5 cm) above eggs. Bring to a boil on medium-high. Reduce heat to medium-low. Cover. Simmer for 10 minutes. Drain. Cover eggs with cold water. Change water each time it warms until eggs are cool. Discard shells. Chop eggs.

Cook peas in water in medium saucepan until just tender. Drain. Rinse with cold water until cool. Drain well.

Put next 4 ingredients into large bowl. Add chopped egg and peas. Toss gently.

Sweet And Creamy Dressing: Combine salad dressing, milk and sugar in small bowl. Makes about 1/2 cup (125 mL) dressing. Drizzle over salad. Toss gently. Serve 6.

1 serving: 234 Calories; 15.8 g Total Fat (6.6 g Mono, 3 g Poly, 5.3 g Sat); 97 mg Cholesterol; 13 g Carbohydrate; trace Fibre; 10 g Protein; 306 mg Sodium

Make It A Meal with grilled or broiled beef steak and heat-and-serve garlic bread.

Broccoli Cheese Salad

Tangy, creamy orange dressing and colourful broccoli will brighten any meal!

Bag of fresh broccoli florets	12 oz.	340 g
Water		
Ice water		
SUNSHINE DRESSING		
Salad dressing (not mayonnaise)	1/3 cup	75 mL
Russian (or French) dressing	2 tbsp.	30 mL
Granulated sugar	1 tbsp.	15 mL
Lemon juice	1 tbsp.	15 mL
Dry mustard	1/4 tsp.	1 mL
Sliced fresh white mushrooms	1 cup	250 mL
Grated medium Cheddar cheese	1 cup	250 mL
Green onions, sliced	4	4

Cook broccoli in water in large saucepan until tender-crisp. Drain. Immediately plunge into ice water in large bowl. Let stand for about 5 minutes until cold. Drain well. Transfer to separate large bowl.

Sunshine Dressing: Combine first 5 ingredients in small bowl. Let stand for about 5 minutes until sugar is dissolved. Stir well. Makes about 1/2 cup (125 mL) dressing. Drizzle over broccoli.

Add remaining 3 ingredients. Toss well. Serves 4.

1 serving: 295 Calories; 25.1 g Total Fat (9.9 g Mono, 6.1 g Poly, 7.9 g Sat); 37 mg Cholesterol; 10 g Carbohydrate; 1 g Fibre; 9 g Protein; 370 mg Sodium

Make It A Meal with grilled or broiled pork chops or chicken breast halves and warm buns.

Paré Pointer
Will the straight and narrow path ever require a four-lane highway?

Spinach Avocado Salad

A rich salad you won't soon forget. So very good!

WARM MUSTARD VINAIGRETTE

Olive (or cooking) oil	3 tbsp.	50 mL
Dijon mustard (with whole seeds)	2 tsp.	10 mL
Maple (or maple-flavoured) syrup	2 tsp.	10 mL
White wine vinegar	1 1/2 tsp.	7 mL
Salt	1/4 tsp.	1 mL
Fresh spinach leaves, lightly packed	5 cups	1.25 L
Ripe medium avocados, sliced	2	2
Sun-dried tomatoes in oil, drained and sliced	1/2 cup	125 mL
Toasted pecan pieces (see Tip, page 46)	1/3 cup	75 mL
Goat (chèvre) cheese, cut up	2 1/2 oz.	70 g

Warm Mustard Vinaigrette: Combine first 5 ingredients in small saucepan. Heat and stir on low until warm. Remove from heat. Makes about 1/4 cup (60 mL) vinaigrette.

Put remaining 5 ingredients into large bowl. Toss gently. Stir dressing. Drizzle over salad. Toss gently. Serves 6.

1 serving: 292 Calories; 26.5 g Total Fat (15.8 g Mono, 3.4 g Poly, 5.7 g Sat); 9 mg Cholesterol; 12 g Carbohydrate; 3 g Fibre; 6 g Protein; 257 mg Sodium

Make It A Meal with fresh tortellini or ravioli, cooked according to package directions and served with your favourite pasta sauce.

Paré Pointer

The walls are so thin, you can hear the rent going up.

Pineapple Shrimp Soup

Sweet and sour soup gently accented with ginger. An enticing combination.

Frozen uncooked medium shrimp (peeled, deveined), thawed	1 lb.	454 g
Soy sauce	1 tbsp.	15 mL
Granulated sugar	1 tbsp.	15 mL
Garlic cloves, minced (or 1/2 tsp., 2 mL, powder)	2	2
Finely grated, peeled gingerroot (or 1/4 tsp., 1 mL, ground ginger)	1 tsp.	5 mL
Pepper	1/2 tsp.	2 mL
Cooking oil	2 tsp.	10 mL
Medium onion, cut into 12 wedges	1	1
Prepared chicken broth	4 cups	1 L
Can of pineapple tidbits (with juice)	14 oz.	398 mL
Medium tomatoes, quartered, seeds removed, diced	2	2
Green onions, cut into 1 inch (2.5 cm) pieces	2	2
Finely shredded basil (or 1 tbsp., 15 mL, dried)	1/4 cup	60 mL
Chopped fresh cilantro or parsley	2 tbsp.	30 mL

Put first 6 ingredients into medium bowl. Stir gently until shrimp are coated. Heat wok or Dutch oven on medium-high. Add shrimp mixture. Stir-fry for 1 to 2 minutes until shrimp just start to turn pink. Transfer to medium bowl. Set aside.

Heat cooking oil in same wok. Add onion wedges. Stir-fry for about 2 minutes until starting to soften.

Add broth and pineapple with juice. Bring to a boil. Reduce heat to medium. Cover. Simmer for 5 minutes, stirring occasionally, to blend flavours.

Add remaining 4 ingredients. Heat and stir for about 5 minutes until heated through. Add shrimp mixture. Stir for about 1 minute until heated through. Makes about 8 cups (2 L).

(continued on next page)

1 cup (250 mL): 129 Calories; 2.8 g Total Fat (1.2 g Mono, 0.9 g Poly, 0.5 g Sat); 65 mg Cholesterol; 14 g Carbohydrate; 1 g Fibre; 12 g Protein; 608 mg Sodium

Make It A Meal with heat-and-serve spring rolls or egg rolls (available in your grocer's freezer) cooked according to package directions and served with plum sauce for dipping.

Chicken Pasta Soup

Everyone loves chicken soup. A standard in any cook's repertoire.

Cooking oil	1 tsp.	5 mL
Finely chopped onion	1 cup	250 mL
Lean ground chicken	1/2 lb.	225 g
Finely chopped celery	1/4 cup	60 mL
Precooked bacon slices, diced	4	4
Water	5 cups	1.25 L
Chicken bouillon powder	1 tbsp.	15 mL
Pepper	1/4 tsp.	1 mL
Frozen mixed vegetables	1 cup	250 mL
Tiny shell (or other very small) pasta	1/2 cup	125 mL
Parsley flakes (or 4 tsp., 20 mL, chopped fresh parsley)	1 tsp.	5 mL

Heat cooking oil in large frying pan on medium-high. Add next 4 ingredients. Scramble-fry for 5 to 10 minutes, stirring occasionally, until ground chicken is no longer pink and onion is softened. Drain.

Combine next 3 ingredients in large saucepan. Bring to a boil on medium-high.

Add chicken mixture, mixed vegetables and pasta. Stir. Cover. Bring to a boil. Reduce heat to medium-low. Simmer for about 10 minutes, stirring occasionally, until pasta is tender but firm.

Add parsley. Stir. Makes about 7 cups (1.75 L).

1 cup (250 mL): 145 Calories; 7.3 g Total Fat (1.4 g Mono, 0.6 g Poly, 0.8 g Sat); 3 mg Cholesterol; 11 g Carbohydrate; 1 g Fibre; 9 g Protein; 375 mg Sodium

Make It A Meal with grilled cheese sandwiches made with sharp Cheddar cheese and whole grain bread.

Thai Chicken Noodle Soup

A spicy soup that's perfect for a cold winter's day.

Boneless, skinless chicken breast half, cut into 1/2 inch (12 mm) cubes	4 – 6 oz.	113 – 170 g
Garlic clove, minced (or 1/4 tsp., 1 mL, powder)	1	1
Chili paste (sambal oelek)	2 tsp.	10 mL
Cooking oil	2 tsp.	10 mL
Peanut butter	2 tbsp.	30 mL
Cans of condensed chicken broth (10 oz., 284 mL, each)	2	2
Water	2 cups	500 mL
Coconut milk (or reconstituted from powder)	1 cup	250 mL
Lime juice	2 tbsp.	30 mL
Oriental steam-fried noodles, broken up	2 1/2 oz.	70 g
Grated carrot	1/4 cup	60 mL
Green onion, sliced	1	1
Fish sauce	1 tbsp.	15 mL
Pepper, sprinkle		
Chopped fresh cilantro or parsley, for garnish (optional)		

Put chicken, garlic and chili paste into small bowl. Stir until chicken is coated.

Heat cooking oil in large saucepan on medium. Add chicken mixture. Heat and stir for 2 to 3 minutes until outside of chicken turns white.

Add peanut butter. Heat and stir for about 1 minute until combined.

Add next 4 ingredients. Stir. Cover. Bring to a boil on medium-high.

(continued on next page)

Add noodles and carrot. Stir. Reduce heat to medium-low. Cover. Simmer for about 5 minutes, stirring occasionally, until noodles are tender but firm.

Add next 3 ingredients. Stir. Cover. Simmer for 5 minutes, stirring occasionally, to blend flavours.

Garnish individual servings with cilantro. Makes about 6 1/2 cups (1.6 L).

1 cup (250 mL): 188 Calories; 13.3 g Total Fat (3 g Mono, 1.5 g Poly, 8 g Sat); 17 mg Cholesterol; 7 g Carbohydrate; 1 g Fibre; 12 g Protein; 773 mg Sodium

Pictured on page 143 and on back cover.

Make It A Meal with heat-and-serve green onion cakes (available in your grocer's freezer) cooked according to package directions and served with chili paste (sambal oelek) for dipping.

Paré Pointer

Even when tailors get tired, they press on.

Lemon Lentil Soup

A fragrant soup with tangy, creamy broth.
A feast for the eyes as well as the palate!

Cooking oil	1 tbsp.	15 mL
Chopped onion	1 1/2 cups	375 mL
Chopped carrot	1 1/2 cups	375 mL
Curry powder	1 1/2 tbsp.	25 mL
Prepared vegetable (or chicken) broth	6 cups	1.5 L
Can of lentils, rinsed and drained	19 oz.	540 mL
Can of coconut milk	14 oz.	398 mL
Bay leaves	2	2
Fresh spinach leaves, lightly packed	2 cups	500 mL
Lemon juice	2 tbsp.	30 mL
Salt	1/4 tsp.	1 mL

Heat cooking oil in large pot or Dutch oven on medium-high. Add onion and carrot. Cook for about 5 minutes, stirring often, until onion starts to soften.

Add curry powder. Heat and stir for 1 to 2 minutes until fragrant.

Add next 4 ingredients. Stir. Bring to a boil. Reduce heat to medium. Cover. Simmer for about 5 minutes, stirring occasionally, until carrot is tender. Discard bay leaves.

Add remaining 3 ingredients. Heat and stir for about 2 minutes until spinach is wilted. Makes about 11 cups (2.75 L).

1 cup (250 mL): 156 Calories; 9.8 g Total Fat (1.4 g Mono, 0.7 g Poly, 6.9 g Sat); 0 mg Cholesterol; 12 g Carbohydrate; 3 g Fibre; 7 g Protein; 592 mg Sodium

Pictured on page 143 and on back cover.

Make It A Meal with pappadum (a wafer-thin East Indian bread made with lentil flour), heated according to package directions. If desired, top pappadum with tomato salsa made with chopped tomato, cucumber and fresh mint. Drizzle with small amounts of lemon juice and olive oil and sprinkle with salt and pepper.

Crab Asparagus Soup

An egg drop-style soup with a sophisticated flavour,
created quickly with easy-to-find ingredients.

Cooking oil	1 tsp.	5 mL
Sliced fresh white mushrooms	1/2 cup	125 mL
Chopped green onion	1/4 cup	60 mL
Garlic clove, minced (or 1/4 tsp., 1 mL, powder)	1	1
Finely grated, peeled gingerroot	1/4 tsp.	1 mL
Pepper	1/4 tsp.	1 mL
Prepared chicken broth	3 cups	750 mL
Fresh asparagus, trimmed of tough ends, cut into 1 inch (2.5 cm) pieces	1/2 lb.	225 g
Can of crabmeat, drained, cartilage removed, flaked	6 oz.	170 g
Cornstarch	2 tsp.	10 mL
Soy sauce	2 tsp.	10 mL
Hoisin sauce	2 tsp.	10 mL
Large egg	1	1
Water	1 tbsp.	15 mL

Heat cooking oil in medium saucepan on medium. Add next 5 ingredients. Cook for 5 to 10 minutes, stirring often, until onion is softened.

Add broth. Stir. Bring to a boil on medium-high.

Add asparagus and crabmeat. Cover. Reduce heat to medium. Boil gently for about 5 minutes until asparagus is tender-crisp.

Combine next 3 ingredients in small cup. Add to soup. Heat and stir for about 1 minute until boiling and slightly thickened.

Beat egg and water with fork in same small cup. Add to soup in thin stream, stirring constantly. Makes about 4 1/2 cups (1.1 L).

1 cup (250 mL): 119 Calories; 3.7 g Total Fat (1.5 g Mono, 0.9 g Poly, 0.8 g Sat); 79 mg Cholesterol;
8 g Carbohydrate; 1 g Fibre; 14 g Protein; 900 mg Sodium

Make It A Meal with heat-and-serve spring rolls or egg rolls (available in your grocer's freezer) cooked according to package directions and served with plum sauce for dipping.

Spanish Black Bean Soup

A dark, rich and filling soup. Great with warm buns on the side.

Cans of black beans (19 oz., 540 mL, each), rinsed and drained	2	2
Medium salsa	1/2 cup	125 mL
Low-sodium prepared chicken broth	3 1/2 cups	875 mL
Tomato paste (see Tip, page 75)	3 tbsp.	50 mL
Cooking oil	2 tsp.	10 mL
Chopped Spanish onion	1 cup	250 mL
Chopped cooked ham	1/2 cup	125 mL
Dry sherry	1/4 cup	60 mL
Dried thyme	1/2 tsp.	2 mL
Bay leaf	1	1
Granulated sugar	1 tsp.	5 mL
Ground coriander	1/2 tsp.	2 mL
Sour cream, for garnish		

Process beans and salsa in blender or food processor until smooth. Transfer to large bowl.

Add broth and tomato paste. Stir well. Set aside.

Heat cooking oil in large pot or Dutch oven on medium. Add onion and ham. Cook for 5 to 10 minutes, stirring often, until onion is softened.

Add next 5 ingredients. Heat and stir for about 1 minute until liquid is evaporated. Add bean mixture. Stir. Bring to a boil on medium-high. Reduce heat to medium-low. Simmer, uncovered, for 8 minutes, stirring occasionally, to blend flavours. Discard bay leaf.

Garnish individual servings with sour cream. Makes about 7 cups (1.75 L).

1 cup (250 mL): 161 Calories; 2.9 g Total Fat (1.3 g Mono, 0.8 g Poly, 0.6 g Sat); 6 mg Cholesterol; 23 g Carbohydrate; 4 g Fibre; 11 g Protein; 703 mg Sodium

Make It A Meal with a salad of chopped tomato, crumbled feta cheese and sliced red onion drizzled with a herb vinaigrette. Serve with crusty rolls.

Tomato Tortellini Soup

A rich, attractive tomato and herb soup.
Tender tortellini rounds out the Italian flavour.

Chopped onion	1/2 cup	125 mL
Bacon slices, diced	2	2
Garlic clove, minced (or 1/4 tsp., 1 mL, powder)	1	1
Prepared chicken (or vegetable) broth	4 cups	1 L
Can of diced tomatoes (with juice)	14 oz.	398 mL
Package of fresh beef (or cheese) tortellini	12 1/2 oz.	350 g
Basil pesto	1 tbsp.	15 mL
Balsamic vinegar	1 tsp.	5 mL
Brown sugar, packed	1 tsp.	5 mL
Salt	1/4 tsp.	1 mL
Pepper	1/8 tsp.	0.5 mL

Cook onion, bacon and garlic in large pot or Dutch oven on medium-high for 5 to 10 minutes, stirring often, until onion is softened and bacon is crisp. Drain.

Add broth and tomatoes with juice. Stir. Bring to a boil.

Add tortellini. Stir. Reduce heat to medium. Boil gently, partially covered, for about 5 minutes, stirring occasionally until tortellini is tender but firm.

Add remaining 5 ingredients. Heat and stir for 1 minute to blend flavours. Makes about 7 cups (1.75 L).

1 cup (250 mL): 164 Calories; 6.8 g Total Fat (1.3 g Mono, 0.4 g Poly, 0.7 g Sat); 32 mg Cholesterol; 15 g Carbohydrate; 1 g Fibre; 10 g Protein; 804 mg Sodium

Make It A Meal with open-face onion buns topped with grated mozzarella cheese and dried herbs. Broil in oven until the cheese is melted. Serve with fresh veggies and dip.

Paré Pointer
You can tell a hockey referee is happy. He whistles while he works.

Curried Lentil Beef Soup

Hearty, fragrant and just spicy enough. Yum!

Cooking oil	1 tbsp.	15 mL
Minute (or fast-fry) steak, thinly sliced (see Tip, page 13)	1/2 lb.	225 g
Chopped onion	1 1/2 cups	375 mL
Curry paste	2 tbsp.	30 mL
Prepared beef broth	6 cups	1.5 L
Can of lentils, rinsed and drained	19 oz.	540 mL
Frozen mixed vegetables	1 1/2 cups	375 mL
Pepper, sprinkle		

Heat cooking oil in large pot or Dutch oven on medium-high. Add steak. Cook for 4 to 5 minutes, stirring occasionally, until browned.

Add onion and curry paste. Heat and stir for 1 minute until fragrant.

Add broth and lentils. Stir. Bring to a boil. Reduce heat to medium-low. Cover. Simmer for 5 minutes, stirring occasionally, to blend flavours.

Add mixed vegetables and pepper. Stir. Bring to a boil on high. Reduce heat to medium. Cover. Simmer for about 5 minutes until vegetables are tender. Makes about 9 cups (2.25 L).

1 cup (250 mL): 165 Calories; 7.5 g Total Fat (3.5 g Mono, 1.1 g Poly, 2.1 g Sat); 13 mg Cholesterol; 14 g Carbohydrate; 3 g Fibre; 11 g Protein; 656 mg Sodium

Make It A Meal with bread sticks or a warm loaf of crusty bread.

1. Quickest Cioppino, page 43
2. Thai Chicken Noodle Soup, page 136
3. Lemon Lentil Soup, page 138

Props courtesy of: Danesco Inc.
Totally Bamboo

Thai Curry Turkey Wraps

Rich, tasty fillings smothered in a spicy curry mayonnaise—
all wrapped up for lunch. So good!

Mayonnaise	1/2 cup	125 mL
Red curry paste	1 tbsp.	15 mL
Flour tortillas (9 inch, 22 cm, diameter)	4	4
Deli smoked turkey	14 oz.	395 g
Deli Swiss cheese slices (about 4 oz., 113 g)	4	4
Fresh spinach leaves, lightly packed	2 cups	500 mL
Ripe medium avocados, sliced	2	2

Combine mayonnaise and curry paste in small bowl. Spread on each tortilla, almost to edge.

Divide and layer remaining 4 ingredients, in order given, across centre of each tortilla. Fold sides over filling. Roll up from bottom to enclose. Makes 4 wraps.

1 wrap: 570 Calories; 31.3 g Total Fat (14.3 g Mono, 5.1 g Poly, 9 g Sat); 98 mg Cholesterol; 32 g Carbohydrate; 5 g Fibre; 42 g Protein; 352 mg Sodium

Make It A Meal with a hearty heat-and-serve bean soup or minestrone.

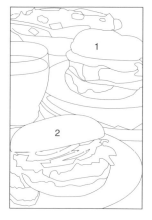

1. Chicken Bacon Burgers, page 146
2. Italian Turkey Burgers, page 147

Chicken Bacon Burgers

Colourful chicken burgers loaded with tasty toppings will please the whole family.

Boneless, skinless chicken breast halves (4 – 6 oz., 113 – 170 g, each)	4	4
Salt, sprinkle		
Pepper, sprinkle		
Cooking oil	2 tsp.	10 mL
Mango chutney	1/4 cup	60 mL
Salad dressing (or mayonnaise)	3 tbsp.	50 mL
Kaiser rolls, split and toasted (buttered, optional)	4	4
Fresh spinach leaves, lightly packed	1 cup	250 mL
Process Swiss cheese slices (about 4 oz., 113 g)	4	4
Tomato slices	4	4
Precooked bacon slices	8	8

Place 1 chicken breast half between 2 sheets of waxed paper. Pound with meat mallet to about 1/2 inch (12 mm) thickness. Repeat with remaining chicken breast halves. Sprinkle both sides of each with salt and pepper.

Heat cooking oil in large frying pan on medium. Add chicken. Cook for 8 to 10 minutes per side until no longer pink inside.

Combine chutney and salad dressing in small cup. Spread on both halves of each roll.

Arrange spinach leaves on top of chutney mixture on bottom half of each roll. Set aside.

Put 1 cheese slice and 1 tomato slice on top of each chicken breast half in pan. Reduce heat to low. Cover. Cook for 2 to 3 minutes until cheese is melted.

Heat precooked bacon according to package directions until crisp. Place 1 chicken breast half on top of spinach on each roll. Top with 2 bacon slices. Cover with top halves of rolls. Makes 4 burgers.

1 burger: 597 Calories; 26.7 g Total Fat (10.8 g Mono, 5 g Poly, 8.7 g Sat); 121 mg Cholesterol; 38 g Carbohydrate; 2 g Fibre; 49 g Protein; 1020 mg Sodium

(continued on next page)

Pictured on page 144.

Make It A Meal with a quick and easy Caesar salad kit (available in your grocer's produce department).

Italian Turkey Burgers

These juicy seasoned burgers, accented with sun-dried tomato pesto, are sure to be a hit!

Fresh bread crumbs	1/3 cup	75 mL
Finely chopped green onion	1/4 cup	60 mL
Soy sauce	1 tbsp.	15 mL
Italian seasoning	1 tsp.	5 mL
Lean ground turkey	1 lb.	454 g
Salad dressing (or mayonnaise)	1/3 cup	75 mL
Sun-dried tomato pesto	2 tbsp.	30 mL
Hamburger buns, split (buttered, optional)	6	6
Mixed salad greens, lightly packed	1 cup	250 mL
Thinly sliced red onion	1/3 cup	75 mL

Preheat two-sided grill (see Note). Combine first 4 ingredients in medium bowl. Add ground turkey. Mix well. Divide and shape into six 4 to 5 inch (10 to 12.5 cm) diameter patties. Cook on greased grill for 5 to 7 minutes until no longer pink inside.

Combine salad dressing and pesto in small cup. Spread on both halves of each bun. Place 1 patty on bottom half of each.

Divide and layer salad greens and red onion on top of each patty. Cover with top halves of buns. Makes 6 burgers.

1 burger: 361 Calories; 16.9 g Total Fat (7.8 g Mono, 4.6 g Poly, 3 g Sat); 60 mg Cholesterol; 31 g Carbohydrate; 2 g Fibre; 20 g Protein; 689 mg Sodium

Pictured on page 144.

Note: Patties may be broiled in oven. Place on greased broiler pan. Broil about 4 inches (10 cm) from heat in oven for about 3 minutes per side until no longer pink inside.

Make It A Meal with a salad of sliced tomatoes, grated bocconcini or mozzarella cheese and chopped fresh basil drizzled with a balsamic vinaigrette.

Grilled Chicken Burritos

Everyone will surely love the mild Southwestern flavours
of these bountiful burritos.

Bacon slices, diced	6	6
Sliced fresh white mushrooms	2 cups	500 mL
Chopped onion	1 cup	250 mL
Chopped cooked chicken	4 cups	1 L
Can of kernel corn, drained	12 oz.	341 mL
Jar of taco sauce	7 1/2 oz.	215 mL
Grated sharp Cheddar cheese	1 1/2 cups	375 mL
Flour tortillas (9 inch, 22 cm, diameter)	6	6

Preheat electric grill for 5 minutes or gas barbecue to medium. Cook bacon in large frying pan on medium-high until almost crisp. Drain, reserving 1 tbsp. (15 mL) drippings in pan.

Add mushrooms and onion. Cook for 5 to 10 minutes, stirring often, until onion is softened and bacon is crisp.

Add chicken, corn and taco sauce. Stir. Reduce heat to medium. Cook, uncovered, for about 5 minutes, stirring occasionally until heated through.

Sprinkle cheese across centre of each tortilla. Spoon chicken mixture onto cheese. Fold sides over filling. Roll up from bottom to enclose. Spray each burrito with cooking spray. Cook on greased grill (see Note) for about 6 minutes, turning 1/4 turn every 1 1/2 minutes until grill marks appear and cheese is melted. Makes 6 burritos.

1 burrito: 509 Calories; 22.8 g Total Fat (8 g Mono, 3.4 g Poly, 9.7 g Sat); 112 mg Cholesterol; 36 g Carbohydrate; 4 g Fibre; 40 g Protein; 769 mg Sodium

Note: If preferred, place burritos on greased baking sheet. Bake in 400°F (205°C) oven for about 10 minutes, turning burritos at halftime, until golden and cheese is melted.

Make It A Meal with a salad of romaine lettuce, chopped tomato, sliced green onion, red pepper and avocado drizzled with a ranch-style dressing.

Turkey Taco Wraps

These meal-size soft tacos are filled with good taste!
Creamy avocado mixed with salsa is the delicious secret.

Cooking oil	2 tsp.	10 mL
Lean ground turkey	1 lb.	454 g
Water	1/4 cup	60 mL
Envelope of taco seasoning	1 1/4 oz.	35 g
Ripe medium avocado, cut up	1	1
Sour cream	1/3 cup	75 mL
Salsa	1/4 cup	60 mL
Flour tortillas (9 inch, 22 cm, diameter)	4	4
Grated Monterey Jack cheese	1 cup	250 mL
Romaine lettuce leaves, cut crosswise into thin strips	4	4

Heat cooking oil in medium frying pan on medium-high. Add ground turkey. Scramble-fry for 5 to 10 minutes until no longer pink. Drain.

Add water and taco seasoning. Heat and stir for 1 minute to blend flavours. Remove from heat. Cover to keep warm.

Mash avocado with fork in medium bowl. Add sour cream and salsa. Mix well. Spread evenly on each tortilla, almost to edge. Spoon turkey mixture across centre of each tortilla.

Sprinkle cheese over turkey mixture. Scatter lettuce over cheese. Fold sides over filling. Roll up from bottom to enclose. Makes 4 wraps.

1 wrap: 590 Calories; 36 g Total Fat (14.8 g Mono, 5.8 g Poly, 12.1 g Sat); 119 mg Cholesterol; 32 g Carbohydrate; 4 g Fibre; 36 g Protein; 1481 mg Sodium

Make It A Meal with coleslaw mix and grated carrot tossed with a coleslaw dressing.

Measurement Tables

Throughout this book measurements are given in Conventional and Metric measure. To compensate for differences between the two measurements due to rounding, a full metric measure is not always used. The cup used is the standard 8 fluid ounce. Temperature is given in degrees Fahrenheit and Celsius. Baking pan measurements are in inches and centimetres as well as quarts and litres. An exact metric conversion is given below as well as the working equivalent (Metric Standard Measure).

Spoons

Conventional Measure	Metric Exact Conversion Millilitre (mL)	Metric Standard Measure Millilitre (mL)
1/8 teaspoon (tsp.)	0.6 mL	0.5 mL
1/4 teaspoon (tsp.)	1.2 mL	1 mL
1/2 teaspoon (tsp.)	2.4 mL	2 mL
1 teaspoon (tsp.)	4.7 mL	5 mL
2 teaspoons (tsp.)	9.4 mL	10 mL
1 tablespoon (tbsp.)	14.2 mL	15 mL

Cups

Conventional Measure	Metric Exact Conversion Millilitre (mL)	Metric Standard Measure Millilitre (mL)
1/4 cup (4 tbsp.)	56.8 mL	60 mL
1/3 cup (5 1/3 tbsp.)	75.6 mL	75 mL
1/2 cup (8 tbsp.)	113.7 mL	125 mL
2/3 cup (10 2/3 tbsp.)	151.2 mL	150 mL
3/4 cup (12 tbsp.)	170.5 mL	175 mL
1 cup (16 tbsp.)	227.3 mL	250 mL
4 1/2 cups	1022.9 mL	1000 mL (1 L)

Dry Measurements

Conventional Measure Ounces (oz.)	Metric Exact Conversion Grams (g)	Metric Standard Measure Grams (g)
1 oz.	28.3 g	28 g
2 oz.	56.7 g	57 g
3 oz.	85.0 g	85 g
4 oz.	113.4 g	125 g
5 oz.	141.7 g	140 g
6 oz.	170.1 g	170 g
7 oz.	198.4 g	200 g
8 oz.	226.8 g	250 g
16 oz.	453.6 g	500 g
32 oz.	907.2 g	1000 g (1 kg)

Oven Temperatures

Fahrenheit (°F)	Celsius (°C)
175°	80°
200°	95°
225°	110°
250°	120°
275°	140°
300°	150°
325°	160°
350°	175°
375°	190°
400°	205°
425°	220°
450°	230°
475°	240°
500°	260°

Pans

Conventional Inches	Metric Centimetres
8x8 inch	20x20 cm
9x9 inch	22x22 cm
9x13 inch	22x33 cm
10x15 inch	25x38 cm
11x17 inch	28x43 cm
8x2 inch round	20x5 cm
9x2 inch round	22x5 cm
10x4 1/2 inch tube	25x11 cm
8x4x3 inch loaf	20x10x7.5 cm
9x5x3 inch loaf	22x12.5x7.5 cm

Casseroles

CANADA & BRITAIN Standard Size Casserole	Exact Metric Measure	UNITED STATES Standard Size Casserole	Exact Metric Measure
1 qt. (5 cups)	1.13 L	1 qt. (4 cups)	900 mL
1 1/2 qts. (7 1/2 cups)	1.69 L	1 1/2 qts. (6 cups)	1.35 L
2 qts. (10 cups)	2.25 L	2 qts. (8 cups)	1.8 L
2 1/2 qts. (12 1/2 cups)	2.81 L	2 1/2 qts. (10 cups)	2.25 L
3 qts. (15 cups)	3.38 L	3 qts. (12 cups)	2.7 L
4 qts. (20 cups)	4.5 L	4 qts. (16 cups)	3.6 L
5 qts. (25 cups)	5.63 L	5 qts. (20 cups)	4.5 L

Recipe Index

151

152

153

154

155

156

Company's Coming cookbooks are available at retail locations throughout Canada!

EXCLUSIVE mail order offer on next page
Buy any 2 cookbooks—choose a 3rd FREE of equal or lesser value than the lowest price paid.

Original Series — CA$15.99 Canada — US$12.99 USA & International

CODE		CODE		CODE	
SQ	150 Delicious Squares	PB	The Potato Book	SDPP	School Days Party Pack
CA	Casseroles	CCLFC	Low-Fat Cooking	HS	Herbs & Spices
MU	Muffins & More	CFK	Cook For Kids	BEV	The Beverage Book
SA	Salads	SCH	Stews, Chilies & Chowders	SCD	Slow Cooker Dinners
AP	Appetizers	FD	Fondues	WM	30-Minute Weekday Meals
SS	Soups & Sandwiches	CCBE	The Beef Book	SDL	School Days Lunches
CO	Cookies	RC	The Rookie Cook	PD	Potluck Dishes
PA	Pasta	RHR	Rush-Hour Recipes	GBR	Ground Beef Recipes
BA	Barbecues	SW	Sweet Cravings	FRIR	4-Ingredient Recipes
PR	Preserves	YRG	Year-Round Grilling	KHC	Kids' Healthy Cooking
CH	Chicken, Etc.	GG	Garden Greens	MM	Mostly Muffins
CT	Cooking For Two	CHC	Chinese Cooking	SP	Soups
SC	Slow Cooker Recipes	PK	The Pork Book	SU	Simple Suppers
SF	Stir-Fry	RL	Recipes For Leftovers	CCDC	Diabetic Cooking
MAM	Make-Ahead Meals	EB	The Egg Book		**NEW** April 15/07

Cookbook Author Biography

CODE	CA$15.99 Canada US$12.99 USA & International
JP	Jean Paré: An Appetite for Life

Most Loved Recipe Collection

CODE	CA$23.99 Canada US$19.99 USA & International
MLA	Most Loved Appetizers
MLMC	Most Loved Main Courses
MLT	Most Loved Treats
MLBQ	Most Loved Barbecuing
MLCO	Most Loved Cookies

CODE	CA$24.99 Canada US$19.99 USA & International
MLSD	Most Loved Salads & Dressings
MLCA	Most Loved Casseroles
MLSF	Most Loved Stir-Fries
	NEW April 1/07

3-in-1 Cookbook Collection

CODE	CA$29.99 Canada US$24.99 USA & International
QEE	Quick & Easy Entertaining
MNT	Meals in No Time

Lifestyle Series

CODE	CA$17.99 Canada US$15.99 USA & International
DC	Diabetic Cooking

CODE	CA$19.99 Canada US$15.99 USA & International
DDI	Diabetic Dinners
LCR	Low-Carb Recipes
HR	Easy Healthy Recipes
HH	Healthy in a Hurry
	NEW March 1/07

Special Occasion Series

CODE	CA$20.99 Canada US$19.99 USA & International
GFK	Gifts from the Kitchen

CODE	CA$24.99 Canada US$19.99 USA & International
BSS	Baking—Simple to Sensational
CGFK	Christmas Gifts from the Kitchen
TR	Timeless Recipes for All Occasions

CODE	CA$27.99 Canada US$22.99 USA & International
CCEL	Christmas Celebrations

Order **ONLINE** for fast delivery!

Log onto **www.companyscoming.com**, browse through our library of cookbooks, gift sets and newest releases and place your order using our fast and secure online order form.

Buy 2, Get 1 FREE!

Buy any 2 cookbooks—choose a **3rd FREE** of equal or lesser value than the lowest price paid.

Title	Code	Quantity	Price	Total
		$	$	$
DON'T FORGET to indicate your FREE BOOK(S). (see exclusive mail order offer above) please print				

TOTAL BOOKS (including FREE)

TOTAL BOOKS PURCHASED: $

	International	USA	Canada
Shipping & Handling First Book (per destination)	$ 11.98 (one book)	$ 6.98 (one book)	$ 5.98 (one book)
Additional Books (include FREE books)	$ ($4.99 each)	$ ($1.99 each)	$ ($1.99 each)
Sub-Total	$	$	$
Canadian residents add GST/HST			$
TOTAL AMOUNT ENCLOSED	$	$	$

Terms
- All orders must be prepaid. Sorry, no CODs.
- Prices are listed in Canadian Funds for Canadian orders, or US funds for US & International orders.
- Prices are subject to change without prior notice.
- Canadian residents must pay GST/HST (no provincial tax required).
- No tax is required for orders outside Canada.
- Satisfaction is guaranteed or return within 30 days for a full refund.
- Make cheque or money order payable to: **Company's Coming Publishing Limited** 2311-96 Street, Edmonton, Alberta Canada T6N 1G3.
- Orders are shipped surface mail. For courier rates, visit our website: **www.companyscoming.com** or contact us: **Tel: 780-450-6223 Fax: 780-450-1857.**

Gift Giving
- Let us help you with your gift giving!
- We will send cookbooks directly to the recipients of your choice if you give us their names and addresses.
- Please specify the titles you wish to send to each person.
- If you would like to include a personal note or card, we will be pleased to enclose it with your gift order.
- Company's Coming Cookbooks make excellent gifts: birthdays, bridal showers, Mother's Day, Father's Day, graduation or any occasion …collect them all!

☐ MasterCard. ☐ VISA Expiry ___ / ___ MO/YR

Credit Card # _____

Name of cardholder _____

Cardholder signature _____

Shipping Address Send the cookbooks listed above to:
☐ **Please check if this is a Gift Order**

Name: _____

Street: _____

City: _____ Prov./State: _____

Postal Code/Zip: _____ Country: _____

Tel: (___) _____

E-mail address: _____

Your privacy is important to us. We will not share your e-mail address or personal information with any outside party.

☐ **YES! Please add me to your News Bite e-mail newsletter.**

Cookmark

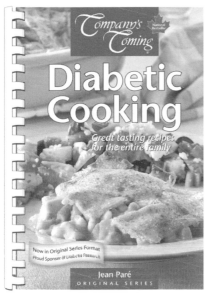

Great-tasting recipes the whole family will love! Made in collaboration with people living with diabetes and their families, *Diabetic Cooking* offers a plethora of smart and delicious eating options—for everyone!

Company's Coming COOKBOOKS®

Quick & Easy Recipes

Everyday Ingredients

Canada's **most popular cookbooks!**